Mindful Leadership

Other Books by Jeffrey L. Buller

Managing Time and Stress: A Guide for Academic Leaders to Accomplish What Matters
The Five Cultures of Academic Development: Crossing Boundaries in Higher Education Fundraising (with Dianne M. Reeves)
Authentic Academic Leadership: A Values-Based Approach to College Administration: Hire the Right Faculty Member Every Time
Best Practices for Faculty Search Committees: How to Review Applications and Interview Candidates
Going for the Gold: How to Become a World-Class Academic Fundraiser (with Dianne M. Reeves)
World-Class Fundraising Isn't a Solo Sport: The Team Approach to Academic Fundraising (with Dianne M. Reeves)
A Toolkit for College Professors (with Robert E. Cipriano)
A Toolkit for Department Chairs (with Robert E. Cipriano)
Academic Leadership Day by Day: Small Steps That Lead to Great Success
Best Practices in Faculty Evaluation: A Practical Guide for Academic Leaders
Building Leadership Capacity: A Guide to Best Practices (with Walter H. Gmelch)
Change Leadership in Higher Education: A Practical Guide to Academic Transformation
Positive Academic Leadership: How to Stop Putting Out Fires and Start Making a Difference
The Essential Academic Dean: A Comprehensive Desk Reference, Second Edition
The Essential College Professor: A Practical Guide to an Academic Career
The Essential Department Chair: A Comprehensive Desk Reference, Second Edition

Mindful Leadership

An Insight-Based Approach to College Administration

Jeffrey L. Buller

ROWMAN & LITTLEFIELD
Lanham • Boulder • New York • London

Published by Rowman & Littlefield
An imprint of The Rowman & Littlefield Publishing Group, Inc.
4501 Forbes Boulevard, Suite 200, Lanham, Maryland 20706
www.rowman.com

6 Tinworth Street, London SE11 5AL, United Kingdom

Copyright © 2019 by Jeffrey L. Buller

All rights reserved. No part of this book may be reproduced in any form or by any electronic or mechanical means, including information storage and retrieval systems, without written permission from the publisher, except by a reviewer who may quote passages in a review.

British Library Cataloguing in Publication Information Available

Library of Congress Cataloging-in-Publication Data

Names: Buller, Jeffrey L., author.
Title: Mindful leadership : an insight-based approach to college administration / Jeffrey L. Buller.
Description: Lanham : Rowman & Littlefield, [2019] | Includes bibliographical references.
Identifiers: LCCN 2018054677 (print) | LCCN 2019000087 (ebook) | ISBN 9781475849158 (Electronic) | ISBN 9781475849134 (cloth) | ISBN 9781475849141 (pbk.)
Subjects: LCSH: Universities and colleges—Administration. | College Administrators—Training of. | Educational leadership. | Mindfulness (Psychology)
Classification: LCC LB2341 (ebook) | LCC LB2341 .B7455 2019 (print) | DDC 378.1/01—dc23
LC record available at https://lccn.loc.gov/2018054677

For Brett Ferrigan and Stephen Perme, who introduced me to meditation and mindfulness.

Contents

Preface		ix
Introduction		xi
1	Mindlessness, Autopilot, and Mindfulness	1
2	Shamatha: Expanding Focus	23
3	Vipassana: Expanding Clarity	47
4	Mantra: Expanding Creativity	69
5	Metta: Expanding Compassion	91
6	Organic, Positive, and Authentic Mindfulness	109
About the Author		123
More about ATLAS		125

Preface

Few topics in recent years have captured the attention of higher education professionals as extensively as mindfulness. Courses and workshops in mindfulness are being introduced at colleges and universities. Pedagogical and administrative conferences frequently have sessions on mindfulness. And administrators are routinely urged to become "more mindful" in their academic leadership.

But what does *mindful leadership* actually mean? How would we recognize the difference between a mindful and a non-mindful academic leader? If we wanted to improve the degree to which we are mindful as leaders, what strategies should we adopt? These are the questions that will be addressed in this book.

With all the changes that are occurring in higher education today, it's increasingly important for administrators to become mindful about what they are doing and why. Failure to do so causes academic leaders to act simply because there is a policy or precedent, regardless of whether that policy or precedent was well considered. Even worse, academic leaders may succumb to the pressures of the moment, placing student recruitment, retention, and the satisfaction of donors ahead of integrity in pedagogy and research.

Mindful leadership is not a panacea. But it is an important ingredient in what distinguishes effective administrators from those who fail. It is also a journey, not a destination: One never reaches a point of saying, "Now I'm perfectly mindful. I can stop here." But it is a journey well worth taking, and I invite you to take it with me.

Introduction

Becoming a mindful leader isn't as easy as reading a book and learning a technique or two. It involves a process of understanding first what mindfulness is and then engaging in the right exercises that will help improve one's mindfulness. Being mindful as a leader involves paying attention to what is happening as it is happening, but it also involves a great deal more. It means learning to lead in a different way, helping people without judging them, guiding people without issuing commands, and assessing situations without unfairly labeling them. As such, mindful leadership is a highly appropriate skill for higher education administrators to have.

Many people assume that mindfulness and meditation are the same thing. That's simply not so. It's rather like assuming that a treadmill and cardiovascular fitness are the same thing. A treadmill is one way of improving your cardiovascular fitness, but there are also other ways. Meditation is just one of many ways of improving your mindfulness. In this book, we'll explore several.

There are many different schools of mindfulness training. No one volume can fully explain them all, but we'll focus on four major approaches that most academic leaders find best suited to the work they do:

- expanding our focus,
- expanding our clarity,
- expanding our creativity,
- and expanding our compassion.

These four approaches serve as the foundation for all the other types of mindful leadership, and, if you master these, you'll find any other approaches you encounter easy to incorporate into your practice.

Because this book is about activity and not just knowledge, each of the first five chapters concludes with exercises to perform before going on to the next chapter. I hope that readers will take these exercises seriously: they're an integral part of what readers can gain from this book, and they'll help prepare readers for the material and activities that will follow. They are, in short, a sort of "homework," but they are homework that I hope you'll find both interesting and revealing.

I'd like to recognize the contributions of Rebecca Peter, who provided substantial editorial and research support throughout this project; David J. Pollay, who gave permission to reprint his Law of the Garbage Truck in chapter 5; Shiful Islam, who gave permission to use his illustration as figure 2.1; and Tom Koerner and Carlie Wall of Rowman & Littlefield, who have been continually helpful and supportive during the creation of this book, as well as many others they have helped me publish over the years.

Jeffrey L. Buller
Jupiter, Florida
November 1, 2018

Chapter 1

Mindlessness, Autopilot, and Mindfulness

Few topics in the twenty-first century have emerged so quickly from relative obscurity to widespread familiarity throughout higher education as has *mindfulness*. A topic once discussed almost exclusively by academics who were interested in meditation or Jon Kabat-Zinn's Mindfulness-Based Stress Reduction (MBSR) approach at the University of Massachusetts Medical School, mindfulness is now the subject of its own academic conferences and a frequent theme for panels and seminars in various disciplines.

The publishing of books related to mindfulness has become a sort of growth industry, and, for those who are interested in improving college administration, a subfield of *mindful leadership studies* has emerged. While nearly all works dealing with mindfulness in an academic setting have focused on elementary and secondary education (see, for example, Brown and Olson 2015, and Shirley and Macdonald 2016), in the corporate world, the topic has received far more attention.

A Mindful Leadership Conference takes place annually (Mindful Leadership Summit n.d.), online training programs in mindful leadership are easy to find (see, for example, the Institute for Mindful Leadership's online course Finding the Space to Lead, 2017 and an online variant of the annual summit mentioned previously, Mindful Leadership Online Conference, n.d.), and the subject has even received what passes today as proof that a topic has entered the mainstream: There is now a book available with the title *Mindful Leadership for Dummies* (Adams 2016).

But despite this seeming omnipresence of mindfulness and mindful leadership as a topic, it still hasn't made deep inroads into how department chairs, deans, provosts, and presidents do their jobs, and many academic leaders aren't quite sure what precisely the terms *mindfulness* and *mindful leadership* mean. Certainly, being more mindful as a leader *sounds* like a good idea, but how would what you *would* be doing differ from what you're doing right now? And is being mindful any different from simply paying more attention to the world around you?

MINDLESSNESS

Have you ever had any of the following experiences?

- You're in a conversation with someone and realize that the last thing you said made absolutely no sense in context. Perhaps it's your birthday, and, as you leave your office, someone calls out "Happy Birthday!" to which you respond "You, too!" even though that person's birthday isn't for four months. Or perhaps you initiated a conversation by saying, "How are you?" to which the person replied, "Fine. How are you?" and you answered (redundantly and awkwardly), "Fine. How are you?"
- You're reading a newspaper, book, or academic article, and you suddenly realize that you can't recall anything you've "read" for the last several pages.
- There's been a power failure for over an hour, and you're forced to find your way around with a candle or flashlight. But every time you enter a new room, you flip on the light switch as though maybe this time the lights will come on.
- You're driving to a destination, arrive, and find that you don't remember anything at all about the trip that got you there. If you're asked about how much traffic you encountered, what you listened to on the radio, or anything you thought about along the way, you wouldn't have an honest answer to provide.
- You're leaving the house in the morning and recognize that you don't remember brushing your teeth, getting dressed, or eating breakfast. And yet, there you are, ready to go to work (even if, occasionally, you later look at what you're wearing and wonder what you were thinking when you chose that outfit).

These are examples of *mindlessness*. When we're acting mindlessly, we're going through the motions of an action even though our thoughts are elsewhere. Sometimes, as in the case of flipping a light switch even though we're aware there is no power, mindless actions are the result of what we sometimes call *muscle memory*. We're responding with muscle memory when we respond in specific—and often quite skilled or detailed—ways without consciously being aware of what we're doing.

Muscle memory is sometimes referred to as a *reflex action*, but a true reflex *can't* be controlled consciously. Sneezing, the patellar response (the original "knee jerk reaction" that occurs when a doctor taps the ligament in someone's knee), and blushing are all reflexes; riding a bicycle, speed typing, and the reactions of those skilled in the martial arts are examples of muscle memory. It's not that you can't fake a sneeze, knee jerk, or blush, but merely that you can't stop this reaction when it occurs. But in the case of riding a bicycle, typing, and the martial arts, we *can* consciously control these actions when we want to.

The connection of most importance for us in this book is that we also *lead* mindlessly at times:

- We're in a meeting, someone asks us a question, and we realize that we have absolutely no idea how to answer it because we haven't been paying attention for several minutes.
- We're so interested in getting to the next goal that we're completely unaware of whether we're effectively achieving our current goal.
- We're so preoccupied with what we'll say next that we're not listening to what other people are saying to us.
- We sign documents without reading them or even knowing what's in them.
- Someone asks us how our semester is going and we respond, "Busy, busy," even though we're probably no busier than the person who asked us the question and almost certainly no busier than we were the previous semester.

Mindless leadership can cause serious problems for a college or university. That document that we signed without reading can commit the institution to spend resources it can't afford or set a precedent that proves problematic in the future. Mindless leadership can also occur when we find ourselves implementing someone else's agenda rather than our own.

Frequently, it's our supervisor who sets our objectives for us, and we find that we're just implementing that person's initiatives, not really leading our units in any meaningful way. But at other times, it can be members of the faculty and staff whose priorities become our own, not because we're consciously trying to be their advocates, but simply because we've stopped paying attention to our programs' larger needs.

Mindlessness can obviously cause us challenges, particularly when we're trying to lead our programs with vision and creativity. But all of us can be mindless from time to time. As a means of gaining some insight into your current level of mindless, habitual response to your environment, complete the following inventory (table 1.1). Read each sentence, and then respond whether that is something that you do (or that describes you) *always*, *often*, *sometimes*, *rarely*, or *never*.

Table 1.1 Mindlessness Inventory

	Always	Often	Sometimes	Rarely	Never
1. Both at work and in my everyday activities, I find myself multitasking.					
2. I spend considerable time worrying or fantasizing about the future.					
3. When I'm introduced to someone new, I tend to forget that person's name unless I repeat it several times or take a business card.					
4. I would describe myself as a creature of habit.					
5. When someone asks me what I did last week, I have to pause several moments to recall.					
6. I forget appointments or activities unless they're written in my calendar.					
7. After eating, I find that I have food or drink stains on my clothing or napkin or discover that I've created more crumbs around my plate than other people.					
8. I get the impression that my friends and coworkers discuss their experiences or problems more with others than they do with me.					
9. I make careless errors when writing, typing, or adding a column of numbers.					
10. I go into another room to get something, but, once I'm there, I've forgotten what it was I wanted.					
11. I find it difficult to remember the meals I've eaten two or three days ago.					
12. When others are speaking to me, my mind may wander off after several minutes.					
13. I spend time thinking about the past, either regretting mistakes I've made or reliving my proudest moments.					
14. While out walking, other people tend to notice things that I don't observe until they mention them.					

(Continued)

Table 1.1 Continued

	Always	Often	Sometimes	Rarely	Never
15. I neglect to thank others for the small favors and kindnesses they do for me.					
16. When I go to a meeting or appointment, I realize that I left home or my office without something important that I will need for the meeting or appointment.					
17. Other people ask me whether I'm obsessive-compulsive.					
18. I reread sentences or paragraphs because I don't understand or can't recall what I just read.					
19. At work, I follow the procedures that have long been in place without questioning why we do things that way or whether there's a better way of doing things.					
20. People tell me that I'm not a good listener.					

After completing the inventory, give yourself five points for each time you answered *Always*, four points for each *Often*, three points for each *Sometimes*, two points for each *Rarely*, and one point for each *Never*. If your score is eighty or above, the amount of time you spend in mindless activity is very high. If your score is fifty-five through seventy-nine, your score falls in the same range as that of most people; while you are actively engaged in most of your day-to-day actions, there's still room for improvement. If your score is forty through fifty-four, you've already gone a long way toward eliminating mindlessness from your daily activity. And if your score is thirty-nine or below, congratulations: You're already among a very small group of people whose level of mindless responses to situations is very low.

Although some of the statements on this inventory are self-explanatory, others may require additional explanation. For example, statements 5, 6, 11, and 18 are fairly obvious from the examples of mindlessness earlier in this chapter. They involve not paying attention in various situations or struggling to remember things that you've done fairly recently.

But why does this inventory ask you whether you're a creature of habit (statement 4) or whether people tend to remark that you may be obsessive-compulsive (statement 17)? As we'll see in a few pages, habits are in and of themselves neither good nor bad. We have habits that can help us (reaching for crisp vegetables when we want a snack) and habits that can harm us (reaching for a cigarette when we're feeling tense). But if we're being honest and say that we're often or always creatures of habit, the implication is that we may not be thinking situations through well enough to determine which of our habits are helpful and which are harmful.

Something similar is likely to be occurring if people often ask us whether we're obsessive-compulsive. The genuine psychological condition of obsessive-compulsive disorder (OCD) can be very serious and have a profound impact on a person's life, but, in day-to-day conversation, people toss around terms like *OCD*, *neurotic*, and *bipolar* in a casual or non-technical manner, unfortunately obscuring the genuine suffering a properly diagnosed psychological condition can cause. So, if people ask you whether you're "a bit OCD," they're probably just noticing that you tend to do things in a specific order or that you're more comfortable following a set routine.

Acting habitually and having a preference for routines do not by themselves mean that you're doing anything wrong. But as part of the overall picture that emerges from all the statements on the inventory, these practices can help clarify the extent to which some of your actions may be more mindless or automatic than you might like.

AUTOPILOT

The term *autopilot* is sometimes used to describe this very type of mindless activity that we've been considering. When we're acting out of habit or muscle memory, we're like a plane that's being guided mechanically without direct intervention by the human pilots (or, in the case of mindlessness, our conscious thoughts).

The assumption is that acting on autopilot is a bad thing. After all, why would you want to perform an action without consciously thinking about it? The answer is that doing so can be a lot more efficient and less exhausting than attempting to focus on every single action we engage in all day long. Todd Kashdan and Robert Biswas-Diener, in *The Upside of Your Dark Side* (2014), observe that too much information is flowing into our brains constantly for us to process it all efficiently. It wouldn't be effective—it wouldn't even be safe—for us to try to think about every single thing we experience.

> Our conscious mind is simply unable to handle the complex, dynamic layers of data flooding us in each moment. One error in processing, and you can step out in front of a fast-moving car, curse in front of your children, let slip a professional secret, burn your hand on the stove, or suffer a million small failures. By

necessity, much of this mental processing happens at the speed of thought below the radar of conscious awareness. (Kashdan and Biswas-Diener 2014, 126)

Moreover, there are even some aspects of life in which mindless reaction actually is a *good* thing. Kashdan and Robert Biswas-Diener describe our instant ability to sense that something doesn't feel right about an unsavory social situation as an example of how our ability to function on autopilot can serve to protect us. They also note that creative ideas more often appear to well up out of our own unconscious thought rather than from intense, active concentration (Kashdan and Biswas-Diener 2014, 128–39).

Coincidentally, I had a rather dramatic confirmation of the phenomenon that Kashdan and Biswas-Diener were describing while writing this chapter. After completing the earlier section on mindlessness, I was consciously aware that the next topic I wanted to address was autopilot and even knew what I wanted to say about this topic. But I couldn't figure out a way to begin or to make a meaningful transition from the previous section. There the situation remained while (untypically for me) I avoided returning to this manuscript for five days and even considered abandoning the whole project.

Finally, I sat down and forced myself to write the first sentence of this section. Ideas still weren't coming, so I decided that working on this manuscript just wasn't in the cards for that day and got up to get a cup of coffee. While preparing the coffee *and not intentionally thinking about the book at all*, suddenly the rest of this section "popped into my head" almost completely developed, and I rushed back to the computer, with my typing barely able to keep up with the thoughts as they emerged.

That's an experience that's familiar to nearly everyone who's ever suffered from writer's block: The harder we try to engage consciously in the process of writing, the more impossible it seems; when we disengage and let our attention drift somewhere else (such as, most famously, while taking a shower or traveling to work), our unconscious minds do the work for us.

These unconscious routines or mental programs our minds use to process information and develop ideas while on autopilot are known as *heuristics*. Several specific kinds of heuristics have been identified.

For example, there's the *representativeness heuristic* by which we assume that our past experience serves as a useful guide to what the future will be like. That's a fairly useful practice if we're assuming that the sun is going to rise in the east tomorrow morning but less useful if we assume that our current romantic partner will cheat on us because the last one did. Like any attempt to determine the next item in a series, the representativeness heuristic becomes more accurate when we're trying to extrapolate from a long, consistent series than from a short or highly inconsistent series.

There's also the *availability heuristic* that we use when we make a judgment on the basis of the information most readily available to us or that first comes to mind. A person who watches news reports that focus on the latest round of natural disasters, terrorist attacks, and violent crimes is much more likely to see the world as a dangerous, threatening place than someone who watches reports of the latest technological breakthroughs, medical advances, and peace accords.

Other types of heuristics exist as well, including the *gaze heuristic* (in which we unconsciously estimate the future trajectory of a moving object based on its past speed, movement, and direction), the *hot-hand fallacy* (that causes us to believe in "streaks" of good or bad luck based on falsely perceived patterns among random events), and *peak-end rule* (in which our evaluation of an entire series of events is defined chiefly by two items in the series: the moment of our most intense emotional response and the last item in the series) (Kahneman, Slovic, and Tversky 2001).

As these examples make clear, heuristics aren't wholly good or bad. They can be helpful when we sense danger in an unfamiliar situation but bad if we gamble more than we can afford because we're "on a streak." And it's precisely at this point that the metaphor of autopilot becomes most useful.

On an aircraft, autopilot can be engaged or disengaged by the pilot depending on whether that type of automatic guidance would be useful. When flying under ordinary conditions, autopilot is useful: The airplane's computer can process far more information than can the pilot's conscious mind, and so engaging autopilot is not merely easier but also safer for all concerned. But in highly complex situations, in which the pilot's experience and human judgment may be of more value than the computer's ability to process information quickly, it may be preferable to disengage the autopilot and fly the plane with the pilot completely in control.

It would be highly desirable, therefore, if we as academic leaders had something similar to this type of intentional control over the way in which we run our programs. We could "engage autopilot" and use heuristics when doing so would be both easier and safer for all concerned. But we could also "disengage autopilot" and make decisions with greater awareness in situations where our experience and professional judgment are of more value. Fortunately, that desirable choice does exist for us in the form of *mindful academic leadership*.

MINDFULNESS

Mindfulness may be defined as *the nonjudgmental awareness of experience as it occurs*. There are three essential criteria contained within this definition:

1. Mindfulness involves *not being immediately judgmental* about the things that happen to us. Notice that word *immediately*. Being mindful doesn't mean that we'll never judge or evaluate our experiences or that we'll regard all experiences as somehow equivalent. It merely means that we'll refrain from a mindless or knee-jerk reaction to something that occurs. Instead, we'll reflect on it more carefully so that we respond to it more appropriately.
2. Mindfulness involves *being aware* of experience. Rather than simply going through the motions of an action while our thoughts stray elsewhere, we are totally engaged with and present in whatever it is we're doing when we're being mindful.
3. Mindfulness involves paying attention to experience *as it occurs*. Reflection on past experience is very useful, and effective academic leaders often review situations to consider how and why they responded as they did and what, if anything, they'd do differently next time. But mindful academic leaders also pay attention to what happens as things are happening. They don't sleepwalk through their days, physically but not mentally "there." Instead, they pay attention to what's going on around them and how what others do and say affects everyone else.

Of these three components, the most important criterion for mindfulness is that it must be *nonjudgmental*. When we judge our experiences, we pigeonhole them or filter them. We label them, and then, rather than paying attention to the experiences themselves, we start paying attention to the labels. A hurtful remark ceases to be a hurtful remark and becomes instead a personal attack or still more evidence that so-and-so is out to get us. We transform our experiences into stories, making it impossible for us to interpret the experience—and not our story about the experience—from that point on. In short, we've exchanged genuine experience for evaluation, and we have no way of knowing whether that evaluation is actually correct.

When we're being mindful, we allow ourselves time to deal with our experiences as experiences. Then, when we have an appropriate degree of distance from what occurred (which may require anything from a few seconds to many years), we can interpret the experience in a manner that is likely to give us the best results. Frequently we think of leadership as the ability to make firm decisions quickly, but the fact is that the speed with which we make decisions does not correlate particularly well with the quality of our results.

A brief thought experiment helps illustrate this point. Imagine that you're a faculty member who, for a number of years, has had a good, productive relationship with Dr. Parker Peyton, a colleague in your discipline. Your conversations with Dr. Peyton have always been cordial, and, although you aren't close friends, you've been to one another's houses a few times.

One day, you're at a faculty meeting with more than twenty other people in attendance. A curricular revision that's very important to you is scheduled for its final vote after more than two years of work. After taking your seat, you overhear Dr. Peyton speaking in a barely concealed whisper to a few people nearby, and the words "idiot," "garbage," and "incompetent" are used. You sense that everyone in the group is quite angry or upset about something.

You're surprised because you've always thought of Dr. Peyton as such a positive person, the sort of colleague who always seems to like everyone. So, you go over to where the conversation is occurring and ask Dr. Peyton what the commotion is all about. Unexpectedly, Dr. Peyton says, "We're talking about you and this useless proposal you keep wasting our time with."

A tense meeting follows, with your curricular proposal being rejected by a two-vote plurality. You're embarrassed and feel that you've spent a lot of time on an idea that, until today, you thought others supported.

As Dr. Peyton is leaving, you ask, "Do you and I need to sit down and talk about this?"

Dr. Peyton replies icily, "I'm not sure we ever need to talk about anything ever again."

Before going on, brainstorm all the possible actions you might take at this point in the story. The goal isn't to identify your best options, the choice you *should* make in this scenario, but merely to list all the choices you *could* make, if you decided to do so. Don't stop until you've generated a list of at least ten very different possibilities. And don't look ahead in this chapter until you've generated your list.

Everyone who engages in this thought experiment will, of course, develop a different list of possible choices. But among the reactions that might appear on your list are the following. You could

- angrily challenge Dr. Peyton on the spot, inquiring why someone whom you regarded as a colleague blindsided you with such a public lack of support.
- calmly question Dr. Peyton on the spot, inquiring why someone whom you regarded as a colleague blindsided you with such a public lack of support.
- go to your supervisor/Human Resources/your union representative and discuss what occurred.
- wait a day or so and then invite Dr. Peyton for coffee or lunch and have a calm conversation about what occurred at the meeting.
- express your feelings in an angry e-mail/letter to Dr. Peyton and send it.
- express your feelings in an angry e-mail/letter to Dr. Peyton and then destroy it.
- calmly express your concerns about what happened in the meeting in a letter or e-mail to Dr. Peyton and send it.

- calmly express your concerns about what happened in the meeting in a letter or e-mail to Dr. Peyton and then destroy it.
- request that another faculty meeting be called to revisit the issue.
- meet one-on-one with other members of the department and try to learn their reasons for voting as they did.
- file a formal grievance against Dr. Peyton.
- wait until Dr. Peyton is not expecting it (such as while walking down the hall or participating in an otherwise calm meeting) and then launch a strong counterattack.
- explore the programs offered by your institution's Employee Assistance Program (if such a benefit exists where you work) and see if it has any resources that can help you deal with this issue.
- regard Dr. Peyton as an enemy and seek to undermine the initiatives of your former colleague as retribution.
- give up going to faculty meetings since they're obviously of no use and your colleagues don't respect you.
- work behind the scenes to discredit Dr. Peyton in the eyes of students and the other members of the department.
- campaign to become department chair so that you can force your proposal through and/or punish Dr. Peyton with undesirable course assignments, limited research funding, and so on.
- reflect on the experience to discover what you may have done to prompt Dr. Peyton's actions against you.
- do nothing.

Your own list is likely to contain variations of several options listed above as well as ideas of your own. Augment your list with any possible actions that appear on this list so that you have a comprehensive list of various options.

Now take your expanded list, and divide it into two categories: those options that are likely to produce a result that you won't end up regretting and those options that are more likely to produce a result that you *will* end up regretting. Look at the two lists that result, and ask yourself the following questions:

- What is the outcome that I most hope to result from whichever option I choose?
- What outcome(s) would probably cause me regret later?
- What possible course of action first came to mind once I read the scenario?
- How long did it take me to come up with the option that I decided was my best choice?
- Nothing in the scenario indicates the gender of Parker Peyton, and the character's name is ambiguous. What gender did I assume this person was? What probably led me to make that assumption?

In the study of mindfulness, we often call the choices people make that lead to results they don't regret *skillful choices* and the choices people make that lead to results they do regret *unskillful choices*. One of the advantages of leading mindfully is that more of our choices are likely to be skillful. You had an example of that benefit in our thought experiment if the choice you decided was best was not the first choice that occurred to you. In certain cases, you may even have been well into your brainstorming process before you came up with what you later regarded as your best choice.

THE MINDFULNESS/AUTOPILOT "SWITCH"

Mindfulness thus helps us make better decisions as academic leaders. But as we saw earlier, there are times when acting on autopilot (i.e., using heuristics) is actually preferable. To understand why this is so, remember what driving was like when you were first learning how to operate a car. You had to be consciously aware of everything: repeatedly checking for vehicles on all sides of your car, keeping an eye on the speedometer, making sure that your hands were properly positioned on the wheel, thinking through all the steps you'd need to take in order to complete a turn, and on and on.

It was even more complicated if you were learning to operate a manual transmission since there were additional processes to consider, sounds to listen for, and synchronized movements of your hands and feet to master. It was fun, but it could also be exhausting, even overwhelming. What was happening is that, due to the novelty of it all, you were driving mindfully at all times.

We can contrast that situation to mindless or inattentive driving when people aren't aware at all of where their vehicle is relative to the traffic or when their attention is occupied by their cell phone, radio, conversations with other passengers, or other distractions. Both situations pose their own threats. Novice drivers have accidents because they're inexperienced and overwhelmed with information and observations that they have to process consciously. Inattentive drivers have accidents because they're oblivious to the information and observations that they need in order to operate their vehicles safely.

But neither of those situations represents the experience of most drivers most of the time. Instead, they drive on autopilot, using subconscious heuristics to operate their vehicles when the weather and traffic is calm and familiar, but becoming more mindful in bad weather, unfamiliar situations, or heavy traffic. We can listen to the radio or engage in conversations without impairing our awareness of the cars around us.

But if we find that we have to make an unexpected detour or suddenly encounter a slick road, we instinctively switch the radio off and cease our conversations so that we can devote our attention fully to these new challenges. Most of us drive so often that we don't even recall developing this habit of switching between mindfulness and autopilot; we just learned to do it by frequently practicing our driving.

Although it may seem as though we're engaged in work these days far more than we're on the road, we simply don't have enough practice in academic leadership for this switch between mindfulness and autopilot to develop naturally. For one thing, most of us began learning how to drive when we were adolescents, decades before we became academic leaders. For another thing, cars and highways change incrementally; higher education changes exponentially and, at times, suddenly.

As every academic leader learns, the strategies that make us effective as college professors don't necessarily make us effective as department chairs, the strategies that make us effective as department chairs don't necessarily make us effective as deans, and so on as we move through the administrative hierarchy.

Moreover, if we change institutions during our careers, we often discover that what worked in one environment isn't effective at all in another environment. Being an academic leader is a lot more complicated than frequently changing the makes of car that we drive or the cities and towns we drive in. It's a lot more like finding out that the controls of the vehicle we're driving today aren't at all in the same place as the car we were driving yesterday, the speed limits have all changed, every street has multiple detours, and all the road signs now have new and unfamiliar symbols.

As a result, we can't expect that the "switch" that allows us to shift between mindfulness and autopilot will simply appear someday if only we engage in academic leadership long enough. In order to practice mindful academic leadership—which includes using autopilot and heuristics when they're useful and avoiding them when they're not—we have to learn how to create and control this "switch." And doing so doesn't occur overnight.

MEDITATION AND MINDFULNESS

The single most common strategy people use to develop mindfulness is meditation. In fact, if you conduct an online search for mindfulness training programs, what you'll find are almost exclusively *meditation* training programs. That occurrence is so common that some people even assume that mindfulness and meditation are the same thing. But they're actually not, and there are lots of misconceptions about what meditation actually is.

- *Meditation is not (necessarily) a religious activity.* The inclusion of meditation among the religious practices of the Hindus, Buddhists, and others make many people believe that meditation is inherently religious in nature. In fact, if you look at the terms and symbols used by many meditation teachers in the West, it's easy to believe that meditation is always a religious practice, possibly even a religious practice associated with specific belief systems. But it's probably better to think of meditation as less similar to something like prayer and more similar to something like fasting. It's very difficult to envision a person praying (at least as that activity is commonly understood) without some type of religious belief. After all, if you don't believe in the supernatural, to whom are you praying? But even though many religions include fasting among their religious practices, people also fast for entirely secular reasons (to lose weight, to break bad eating habits, to improve mental clarity, and so on; for a list of ten entirely non-religious reasons to fast, see Edwards 2017). Meditating to gain better control over your mindfulness is thus like fasting to reset your body clock. You don't have to change religions—or even be religious at all—in order to engage in this activity. It's simply a type of exercise or training.

- *Meditation does not involve going into a trance.* When some people see others meditating, they assume that meditation involves some type of altered mental state that makes people indifferent to or unaware of what's going on around them. But meditation would be a very strange way of trying to improve mindfulness if those who practiced it became unaware of their experience. To the contrary, meditation involves *increasing* people's conscious awareness of what is happening around them, how their actions affect that experience, and why what they do matters. People who meditate don't become cut off from or apathetic to the world. In time, they may become less anxious about situations they can't control, and they may stop beating themselves up about past mistakes that they can't rectify. But that's because they've become more mindful about how the world actually works, not because they've shifted their consciousness to a different plane.
- *Meditation is not about emptying your mind of all thoughts.* One stereotype of a meditation instructor imagines the teacher beginning the lesson by saying, "Now first clear your mind of all thoughts." The idea is that meditation is about sitting around serenely thinking about absolutely nothing at all.
- *Meditation does not require hard concentration.* We often say that we're "meditating on something" when what we mean is that we're directing full and focused attention toward it, we're concentrating on it so hard that we may even furrow our brows and squint in order to "see things more clearly," and we're contemplating it with all of our mental energy. But that type of "meditation" involves *narrowing* our mental focus, not broadening it. It can actually cause us to become less aware of our experience as it occurs. ("What? The fire alarm went off? Sorry. I wasn't paying attention.

I was meditating on how we can get that accreditation report done by next Friday.") The meditation exercises that we'll explore in this book don't require *mental squinting*, that exhausting type of intellectual focus that shuts out everything else but the object of our concentration. As we'll see, they involve allowing the mind to rest on particular aspects of our experience or even all of our experience at once, no brow furrowing required.

- *Meditation is not the only way of developing mindfulness.* As mentioned earlier, many of the websites devoted to mindfulness can leave you with the impression that meditation alone can help people become more mindful or even that meditation and mindfulness are somehow the same thing. But that's simply not the case. Meditation is a practice or an exercise. Just as there are more ways to lose weight than engaging in the practice of fasting and more ways to improve muscle than engaging in the exercise of weight lifting, so are there ways to improve mindfulness that don't involve meditation at all. Because there are plenty of people who have decided that meditation is just not for them—perhaps because, despite assurances, they still view it as a religious activity, perhaps because they dislike the idea of sitting or walking quietly for extended periods of time, or perhaps because they live or work in an environment where it would be all but impossible to sit or walk quietly for an extended period of time—non-meditative alternatives will be mentioned in every chapter. For this reason, you can learn everything you hope to from this book and never meditate once, or you can combine meditative and non-meditative approaches to mindfulness as a way of seeing which types of activities work best for you.

As a practice or exercise, meditation is thus a tool we can use (or not) to accomplish the goal of leading more mindfully. It isn't the goal itself. We learn how to use the recumbent bicycle at the gym not because we're interested in learning how to use a recumbent bicycle *per se* but because it's a tool that helps us improve our cardiovascular health. Similarly, we learn how to meditate not because we're interested in learning how to meditate *per se* but because it's a tool that helps us improve our mindfulness.

If other tools like spin bikes, actual bikes, treadmills, long walks, stair climbing, and so on work better for us or better suit our lifestyles and still improve our cardiovascular health, we're welcome to switch or combine tools. If the other activities and exercises discussed in this book work better for you or suit your lifestyle better and still help you improve your mindfulness, you're welcome to use those instead of or in addition to meditation. Throughout the chapters that follow, remember that this book is not intended to promote meditation necessarily; instead, this book intends to promote mindful academic leadership.

LEADING MINDFULLY

By now it should be fairly clear what mindfulness itself is, but there may still be some lack of clarity about the nature of *mindful leadership*. Is mindful leadership anything more than simply paying attention to what we do when we lead? And if so, shouldn't paying attention just be a requirement for *all* leadership?

To begin to answer these questions, we should recognize that "simply paying attention" as a leader is no small feat. As academic administrators, we're inundated with information on a daily basis. We have an almost unbelievable number of diverse constituencies to serve, and these stakeholder groups become even more varied (and demanding) the higher we rise in the institutional hierarchy.

If you're not yet a president or chancellor, think for a moment of all the different groups—from legislators, board members, and donors through the faculty, staff, and administration to students, community members, and groups with a vested interest—that chief executive officers have to deal with. Each of those groups has its own perspective, its own demands, and its own conviction that its needs are the ones that must be addressed immediately.

It's all but impossible to pay attention to every element in this welter of conflicting pressures simultaneously. And yet that's exactly what presidents and chancellors are required to do, twenty-four hours a day, seven days a week.

Regardless of what your position is as an academic leader, you face your own version of this challenge yourself. You may *want* to pay attention to all the critical information that comes your way, but it doesn't always feel possible. That very predicament can lead to some very serious problems. With people clamoring for instant decisions and instant attention, it can be easy to slip into mindless leadership despite our best intentions. We make decisions merely because a decision has to be made, and we offer people answers merely because they won't stop asking us until we do.

That's why Valerie Brown and Kirsten Olson in *The Mindful School Leader* recommend that administrators recall the acronym STOP whenever they feel they're beginning to get overwhelmed (Brown and Olson 2015, 19). STOP stands for

*S*top
*T*ake a breath
*O*bserve
*P*roceed

A great deal of advice about mindful leadership is just an elaboration of this practice: reminding oneself to switch from autopilot to mindfulness, pay genuine attention to what is occurring, consider the implications of the various choices we are considering, and then move ahead with the best choice we can make using our professional judgment, experience, and training.

Although Brown and Olson intended their advice for pre-college administrators, it works equally well in higher education. Even though we'll see in the chapters ahead that there's a great deal more that department chairs, deans, provosts, and presidents can accomplish by adopting the more advanced techniques we'll explore, even this one initial step toward being more mindful as leaders can help us make more skillful choices as we work to improve our programs.

The website of the Institute for Mindful Leadership provides a useful description of what distinguishes mindful from more traditional styles of leadership:

> A mindful leader embodies leadership presence by cultivating focus, clarity, creativity, and compassion in the service of others. Leadership presence is a tangible quality. It requires full and complete nonjudgmental attention in the present moment. Those around a mindful leader see and feel that presence. (What Is a Mindful Leader? 2017)

That brief paragraph contains so many important elements that, before we continue, it will be useful to pause—or, as Valerie Brown and Kirsten Olson would say, stop, take a breath . . . —and review each of them individually.

First, mindful leadership is closely connected with the notion of *leadership presence*. Administrators with leadership presence truly engage with their stakeholders; they don't view them as means to an end but rather as ends in themselves.

I once worked for a president who, at meetings and social events, would chat with each person briefly and then, if that person wasn't a donor or board member, move on, patting the person on the shoulder as he walked away. The brief touch to the shoulder was intended to give the illusion of friendliness, but it was actually dismissive, not a tap of affection as much as a (thinly concealed) push away. This move, which might be called the *presidential pat-off*, signifies the lack of leadership presence, and it appears to correlate closely with administrators who prove to be unsuccessful after a few years in their positions.

Many people who met either Jackie Kennedy or Bill Clinton said that, when they were talking to you, you felt like you were the most important person in the room. That's because they were truly present and engaged with the people they met. As the Dutch inspirational speaker, trainer, and writer Alexander den Heijer has said, "When I talk to managers, I get the feeling they're important. When I talk to leaders, I get the feeling I'm important."

(Heijer 2016). People have leadership presence not because you know they're there and in command; they have leadership presence because they awaken possibilities in others.

Second, mindful leadership involves the cultivation of focus, clarity, creativity, and compassion. Those four objectives suggest the four meditative and non-meditative strategies that serve as the core of this book. In other words, if the primary goal of mindful academic leadership is to pay better attention to the truly important things we experience as an administrator, then the best way to do that is to increase our awareness, lucidity, inventiveness, and kindness toward others. Each of the four advanced strategies that we explore will be directed toward one of those goals.

Third, mindful leadership is "tangible" and apparent to more people than just the leader alone. You can study things like stress management and work-life balance with the intention of benefiting yourself alone. But mindful academic leadership isn't like that. While it has many personal benefits (such as increasing your ability to be calm in stressful situations), those personal benefits are only a by-product of several larger goals: serving the needs of *all* your stakeholders (not merely the ones who can advance your career), improving the programs under your supervision, and strengthening higher education generally.

Those are lofty and ambitious goals, but they're well within the capabilities of every academic leader who's committed to achieving them. They are also so important that, once you begin to see what's possible through mindful academic leadership, you'll wonder why you ever tried to lead any other way.

KEY POINTS FROM CHAPTER 1

- Mindlessness is the habit of going through the motions of an action without our consciousness being fully engaged.
- Autopilot is the use of heuristics (subconscious decision-making routines) to engage in activities without being aware of how or why various decisions are being made.
- Mindfulness is the nonjudgmental awareness of experience as it occurs.
- Skillful choices lead to results that we don't later regret, while unskillful choices more frequently lead to results we later wish we could undo.
- Meditation is not necessarily a religious activity, doesn't involve going into a trance, doesn't require hard concentration, and isn't the only activity or practice we can engage in to increase our mindfulness.
- Mindful leadership involves paying more attention to what is happening around us in leadership situations and what might result from the choices we make, but it also helps us to cultivate focus, clarity, creativity, and compassion in the service of others.

- Leadership presence is the active and sincere engagement that leaders have with their stakeholders.
- The presidential pat-off is a habit (not limited to university presidents alone) in which a leader ends a conversation with someone by saying a few words of dismissal, patting the person on the shoulder, and walking away. Presidential pat-offs have a strong negative correlation with leadership presence.
- Mindful academic leadership has benefits for the leaders themselves, but, more importantly, it has obvious and tangible benefits for the institution and all the leader's stakeholders.

EXERCISES TO COMPLETE BEFORE PROCEEDING TO CHAPTER 2

1. In addition to the inventory that appears in this chapter, there are a number of very helpful mindfulness inventories and scales available elsewhere. These resources include the Freiburg Mindfulness Inventory (Freiburg Mindfulness Inventory 2013, and Walach, Buchheld, Buttenmuller, Kleinknecht, and Schmidt 2006), the Mindful Attention Awareness Scale (Medvedev, Siegert, Feng, Billington, Jang, and Krägeloh 2016), and the Toronto Mindfulness Scale (Lau et al. 2006). Complete as many of these instruments as you can in order to obtain a baseline reading for your current level of mindfulness. In chapter 6, we'll return to these instruments so that you can determine whether your level of mindfulness has improved due to the strategies discussed in the intervening chapters.
2. Identify a problem or an individual in your work environment that causes you to react in an unskillful manner. Frequently this person or situation will be one that "pushes your buttons" and causes you to respond in a manner that you later regret. Think back to the last time this problem or person caused you to act in a way that later dissatisfied you, and brainstorm two lists similar to those you developed in the Parker Peyton thought experiment in this chapter: What are all the possible choices you could have made? Which choices would you characterize as skillful, and which would you characterize as unskillful? The next time you find your "buttons being pushed" by this problem or individual, remember your list of skillful choices and respond with one of those.
3. Every time that you remember to do so, try to use Valerie Brown and Kirsten Olson's STOP technique (as described above) in high pressure situations for one full week. How difficult do you find it to recall this technique in situations where your stress level has increased? Do you discover that you increase or decrease your use of this technique as the week goes by?

REFERENCES

Adams, J. 2016. *Mindful Leadership for Dummies.* Chichester, UK: Wiley.
Brown, V., and K. Olson. 2015. *The Mindful School Leader: Practices to Transform Your Leadership and School.* Thousand Oaks, CA: Corwin.
Edwards, S. 2017. 10 Reasons to Fast. *How to Be Fit.* Retrieved from http://www.howtobefit.com/10-reasons-to-fast.htm.
Finding the Space to Lead. 2017. *Institute for Mindful Leadership.* Retrieved from https://instituteformindfulleadership.org/finding-space-lead-practical-guide-mindful-leadership-online-course/.
Freiburg Mindfulness Inventory. 2013. *Mindfulness Extended.* Retrieved from http://www.mindfulness-extended.nl/content3/wp-content/uploads/2013/07/Freiburg-Mindfulness-Inventory.pdf.
Heijer, A. 2016. Quotes. *Alexander den Heijer.* Retrieved from https://www.alexanderdenheijer.com/quotes.
Kahneman, D., P. Slovic, and A. Tversky. 2001. *Judgment under Uncertainty: Heuristics and Biases.* Cambridge, UK: Cambridge University Press.
Kashdan, T., and R. Biswas-Diener. 2014. *The Upside of Your Dark Side: Why Being Your Whole Self—Not Just Your "Good" Self—Drives Success and Fulfillment.* New York: Hudson Street.
Lau, M. A., S. R. Bishop, Z. V. Segal, T. Buis, N. D. Anderson, L. Carlson, S. Shapiro, J. Carmody, S. Abbey, and G. Devins. 2006. "The Toronto Mindfulness Scale: Development and Validation." *Journal of Clinical Psychology* 62 (12): 1445–67.
Medvedev, O. N., R. J. Siegert, X. J. Feng, D. R. Billington, J. Y. Jang, and C. U. Krägeloh. 2016, April. "Measuring Trait Mindfulness: How to Improve the Precision of the Mindful Attention Awareness Scale Using a Rasch Model." *Mindfulness* 7 (2): 384–95.
Mindful Leadership Online Conference. n.d. Retrieved from http://mindfulleadershipconference.com.
Mindful Leadership Summit. n.d. *Mindful Leader.* Retrieved from http://www.mindfulleader.org.
Shirley, D., and E. Macdonald. 2016. *The Mindful Teacher* (2nd ed.). New York: Teachers College Press.
Walach, H., N. Buchheld, V. Buttenmuller, N. Kleinknecht, and S. Schmidt. 2006. "Measuring Mindfulness—The Freiburg Mindfulness Inventory (FMI)." *Personality and Individual Differences* 40 (8): 1543–55.
What Is a Mindful Leader? 2017. *Institute for Mindful Leadership.* Retrieved from https://instituteformindfulleadership.org/definitions/.

RESOURCES

Bunting, M. 2016. *The Mindful Leader: 7 Practices for Transforming Your Leadership, Your Organisation and Your Life.* Milton, AUS: Wiley.

Carroll, M. 2008. *The Mindful Leader: Awakening Your Natural Management Skills through Mindfulness Meditation*. Boston: Trumpeter.

Gonzalez, M. 2013. *Mindful Leadership: The 9 Ways to Self-Awareness, Transforming Yourself, and Inspiring Others*. San Francisco, CA: Jossey-Bass.

Kets, M. F. R. 2014. *Mindful Leadership Coaching: Journeys into the Interior*. New York: Palgrave Macmillan.

Marturano, J. 2015. *Finding the Space to Lead: A Practical Guide to Mindful Leadership*. New York: Bloomsbury Press.

Chapter 2

Shamatha

Expanding Focus

According to chapter 1, we should think of meditation as a type of exercise. No one learns how to use a recumbent bicycle for the sake of learning how to use a recumbent bicycle; it's just a tool that helps us achieve some kind of goal, such as losing weight or improving our cardiovascular health. There's one more similarity between meditation and a piece of exercise equipment: You don't achieve that goal simply by using it once or even by using it sporadically. Progress comes when you engage in exercise regularly, perhaps not by doing the same routines every day but by returning to them often enough so that you can make progress.

The same thing is true about meditation. None of the techniques that you'll learn about in this book will produce instant results. In fact, none of them are going to reveal their full advantage for the first several months. The important thing is to continue the practice and to be regular about it.

To make things as easy as possible, this book does not recommend (as some schools of meditation do) that you dedicate half an hour to a technique twice a day or immediately devote a week or more to a meditation retreat. Academic leaders don't have that kind of time. Instead, we're going to explore techniques of building mindfulness that only take a few minutes each time you do them. But the important thing will be that you need to do them every day.

One excellent book on meditation is Victor Davich's *8 Minute Meditation* (2014). In it, Davich argues that, these days, people just don't have time to devote an hour or more each day to a practice that won't pay off for many months (Davich 2014, 16–18). Probably one of the reasons why many people don't stick to a meditation regimen once they start it is the same reason why people don't use their gym memberships once they buy them: They don't see results immediately, and then they get so busy that they slip in their resolve to set aside that half-hour or hour each day.

We're going to try to avoid that pitfall by keeping our meditation sessions short. No matter how full your day is, you can find five minutes to set aside, maybe even ten minutes. The approach we're going to use won't require more from you than that.

STANDARD MEDITATION PREPARATION

We're going to explore four main types of meditation in this book, but your preparation will be the same in each case. A lot of meditation training tells you to adopt a very specific posture and may even expect you to hold your hands in certain positions, called *mudras*. Those guidelines are often based on certain assumptions about how the body works and how energy flows through the body that are irrelevant to mindful academic leadership. (In addition, skeptics wouldn't find any compelling evidence in support of these assumptions anyway.)

The sole principle we'll use with regard to posture is that you should position yourself in such a way as to encourage alertness and discourage the natural tendency to fall asleep when you're still and the room is quiet. For that reason, if the recommended posture doesn't work for you, find one that does. The important thing is to increase your mindfulness, not to follow a set of overly prescriptive guidelines. By that same token, if you have a posture you've learned from a particular school of meditation and want to use it, feel free.

With the goals of comfort and alertness in mind, here are the preparations you should make for each style of meditation that you'll do:

1. Find a chair with a back but no arms. The seat of the chair should be comfortable enough that it doesn't cut off the circulation to your legs or attract your attention when you want to focus your attention elsewhere.
2. Sit on the chair in whatever position you find most comfortable.
3. Rest your hands in a position where you won't be tempted to move them during the meditation. Some people rest their hands loosely in their laps, others place them palm downwards on their upper legs or knees, and still others let them hang loosely at their sides. You may have to experiment a bit to find the position that is most comfortable for you.
4. Either loosely close your eyes or leave them open but with your eyelids and gaze relaxed.
5. Breathe normally.

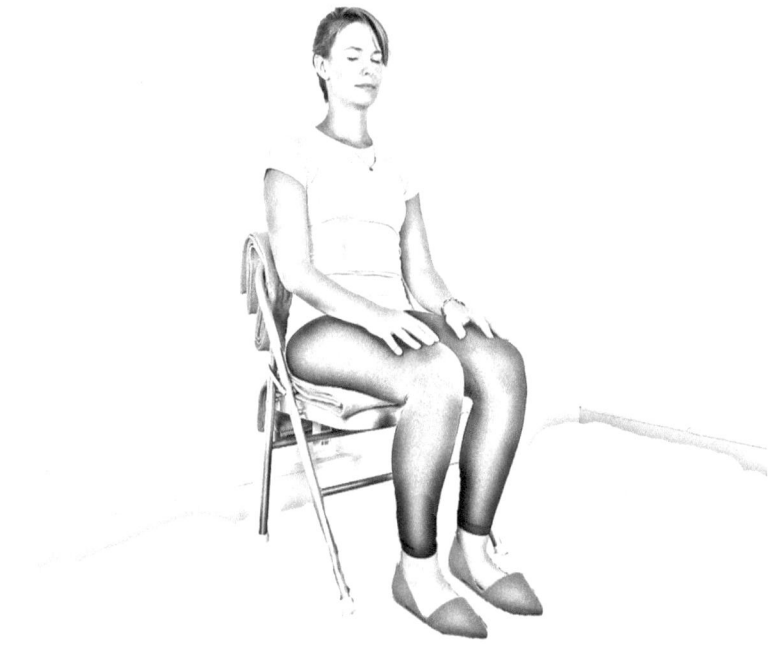

Figure 2.1 Seated Meditation Posture. *Source:* Shiful Islam.

That's it! If you follow these instructions, you may end up seated in a position rather similar to what is illustrated in figure 2.1. But if you end up sitting differently—or even if you prefer to stand, kneel, or lie down—that's perfectly fine as long as you can hold that position while being comfortable but alert throughout the five- to ten-minute meditation sessions that we'll be practicing.

SHAMATHA MEDITATION

Of the four types of meditation that we'll experiment with in this book, we're going to start with a type known as *shamatha* (pronounced SHAH-muh-tuh) *meditation*. There are two very important reasons for beginning with this style. First, it's the type of meditation that most people think of when they hear the word *meditation* (e.g., "just focus on the breath"). Second, it serves as a good prelude to the other three types that we'll consider. As we'll see later on, even some of the meditation schools that emphasize one of the other approaches we'll consider actually begin their training (and at times every meditation session) with shamatha.

Each approach to meditation that we'll explore is a type of *single point meditation*. That is to say, they each involve training the mind to rest its awareness on some single point or object. What's different about each approach to meditation is what that single point is. With shamatha meditation, the single point on which we'll allow our minds to rest is the breath.

The word *shamatha* itself is a Sanskrit term meaning *calm* or *calm abiding*. The name of the approach then is tied to one of the key benefits—actually, as we'll see, it's really a by-product—of this method. Once you've engaged in shamatha meditation for a while (typically after two or three months) you'll notice that you'll come away from your sessions feeling much calmer than you were before you began them. Even before you become aware of this sensation yourself, people who know you well might mention that you seem to be calmer these days or ask what you're doing (or what medication you're trying!) that has relieved you of so much stress.

The stress-relieving aspect of shamatha meditation is the reason why a variation of this approach is used in the Mindfulness-Based Stress Reduction (MBSR) training that was pioneered by Jon Kabat-Zinn and mentioned in chapter 1. For people whose sole interest in meditation is improving their ability to cope with the pressures of work or life, shamatha meditation is a good choice. It requires no equipment, can be done anywhere, and is easy to learn. After you've practiced shamatha for a while, you won't even have to engage in the practice to start feeling calm. As soon as you think, "I'm going to go meditate now," you'll start to feel relaxed.

Although stress reduction is valuable for any academic leader, we're interested in shamatha meditation, not solely for this by-product, but for its primary goal: increasing mindfulness. (In MBSR the emphases are reversed. In MBSR, people become mindful in order to decrease stress. In this book's practice, academic leaders decrease stress in order to become more mindful. Either approach is valid.)

What's important to recognize is that, while meditation is effective in reducing stress, it's also capable of aiding us in many other ways as well. In fact, David Michie, one of the cofounders of the group Organisational Mindfulness, speaks of the overemphasis on the stress-reducing aspects of meditation as the "dumbing down of mindfulness" because it ignores so many other benefits (Michie 2014, 7).

To avoid this tendency, the exercise that we're going to explore in this chapter trains us to become more mindfully and nonjudgmentally aware of experience as it occurs because we will practice being mindfully and nonjudgmentally aware of the breath for short periods of time.

Why the breath and not something else? Well, as we'll see when we examine other techniques, the one-point focus of our meditation practice can be *anything*. But for people who are just beginning to learn about meditation and mindfulness, it's useful to begin by paying attention to the breath for these reasons:

- Our breath is both controllable and autonomous. That is to say, you can control your breath in many different ways. You can take deep breaths, shallow breaths, rapid breaths, slow breaths; you can even hold your breath for a certain amount of time. But when you stop thinking about your breath, you go on breathing anyway. For this reason, it's a perfect example of an activity that we can do either mindfully or mindlessly. It helps remind us that there are a lot of other things we do that we can also do either mindfully or mindlessly although we may not always be aware that that is the case.
- By its very nature, your breath is transitory and momentary. It thus becomes a convenient symbol of the current, fleeting moment. The Japanese practice of gathering with friends and family members to view cherry blossoms each spring is not merely done for social reasons or to have a chance to see something beautiful. It's a chance to see something beautiful *that won't last*, a reminder that youth and even life itself are temporary. They have their season—and then they're gone. On a very small scale, each breath we take is like that. At the moment it occurs, it's vitally important; we literally couldn't live without it. But that moment soon passes, and the air we needed to inhale because it was useful to us must then be exhaled because its oxygen has been depleted. Paying attention to our breath can remind us, therefore, that today's "crisis" often becomes tomorrow's "Now, what was it I was doing yesterday?" It can be a good cue to keep our priorities straight.
- Our breath is one of the ways in which we connect to and interact with the world. The air of our breath comes from outside of us, enters us to become "ours" for a little while, and then returns to the outer world in a cycle that continues throughout our lives. When we increase our mindfulness, we also increase our awareness of this reciprocal relationship we have with the world. We realize that it's not all about us. But it's also not all *not* about us either. We have to be aware that what we do has an impact on others, just as what they do has an impact on us. By becoming more aware of our breath we become more aware of this constant interchange between ourselves and the world that is a key component of mindfulness.
- Breathing has a direct relationship with mood, sometimes as cause and other times as effect. We recognize this relationship instinctively when we notice someone hyperventilating or someone who's nervous and tell them to take a deep breath. In an article appearing in *Science*, a group of researchers discovered that a cluster of neurons in the brain stem, known as the pre-Bötzinger complex, functions essentially as a "breath pacemaker"—at least in mice (Yackle et al. 2017). As the animal becomes calmer,

the complex slows breathing, and, as the animal becomes more excited, the complex speeds breathing. But what was most interesting is that the process also works in reverse: slowing the breath *induces* calm and speeding up the breath *induces* excitement. So, greater awareness of the breath doesn't merely help us become more mindful of ourselves and our environment; it helps us become more mindful of (and in control of) our emotions.

For all these reasons, shamatha meditation provides an excellent introduction to the other mindfulness techniques that we'll explore in this book. Here, then, is what you'll do during a session of shamatha meditation:

1. Complete the standard meditation preparation as described earlier in this chapter.
2. Set a timer for five minutes.
3. Slowly take three deep breaths, paying full attention to every sensation you have while inhaling and exhaling.
4. After exhaling the third breath, return to breathing normally.
5. On each subsequent in-breath, let your attention rest on the fact that you're inhaling.
6. On each subsequent out-breath, let your thoughts go where they may.
7. Continue this process until the timer goes off.

There are a couple of important ideas to remember as you engage in this practice. First, you'll discover periodically that your mind has been wandering and that you haven't been paying attention to your in-breath. You may experience a temptation to feel annoyed and think, "I'm doing this wrong!"

But, actually, the very fact that you realized your mind was wandering proves that you were doing it right. What people sometimes don't realize is that being aware of your in-breath isn't meditating. Okay, that's an overstatement. Being aware of your in-breath isn't the sum total of meditating. Remembering that your thoughts have strayed elsewhere and then *gently, nonjudgmentally guiding them back to awareness of the in-breath* is the meditation. Or, again to avoid overstatement, that's the most important part of the meditation. Don't blame yourself when this happens; you are engaging in the exercise *so that* this would happen.

A lot of guilt has been imposed on meditators by teachers who liken wandering thoughts to *monkey mind*—the tendency of the mind to jump randomly from thought to thought like a monkey jumping randomly from branch to branch—and similar derogatory terms. But these labels get in the way of progress toward mindfulness; they don't promote it.

It's far better to think of your wandering mind as though it were a dear but absentminded friend who strays off every now and then. When you realize what has happened, don't get angry. Instead, rejoice that you've met up again with your good friend, and think, "There you are! I've been looking for you. Why don't you come back here with me, and we'll spend some time together again?" (For a similar idea, see Chödrön 2005, 172.)

Second, don't expect that there will be a blinding flash of insight or that you'll suddenly obtain enlightenment while meditating. That sort of thing happens in books and movies about meditation but rarely, if ever, in real life. And even if it does occur, our goal in this book isn't enlightenment, but mindfulness.

What you're trying to do is train yourself to have more control over your autopilot or mindfulness "switch." That's why the act of calmly restoring your attention to your breath from wherever it has been *is* the exercise. The more you do it, the easier it becomes. And after a few months of practice, you'll find yourself mindfully engaged in everything you do to a much greater extent than you are now. You're not surrendering your autopilot or mindfulness "switch"; you're strengthening it. You'll still have the ability to resort to heuristics whenever that's preferable. But you'll also have greater control over your ability to be mindfully aware of situations when you need to be.

As you continue your practice, reflect occasionally on what occurs during your meditation sessions. Do you find that you're spending longer periods in a state of awareness of your breath, thus reminding yourself to bring your attention back to the present moment less and less often? What thoughts do you have during your out-breaths? Do you notice anything creative or unexpected occurring to you at those times? Do unpleasant or negative thoughts ever arise while you're meditating, such as self-blame, regret, or fear? Could you use the same technique of returning your awareness to the breath or the present moment at other times in your life when these negative thoughts arise?

NON-MEDITATIVE APPROACHES TO SHAMATHA

Even though this book attempts to secularize the practice of meditation and to free it from the New Age trappings that sometimes surround it, there are bound to be readers of this book who reviewed the last few sections and thought, "That's just not for me. I'm not sitting and thinking about my breath or staring at my navel or doing anything like that. That's just not who I am."

That's okay. Fortunately, although meditation is a particularly common and (for most people) enjoyable way of achieving mindfulness, it's not the only way. There are non-meditative practices you can engage in that yield the same results as shamatha meditation. Even if you do want to start a meditation practice, engaging in these activities can help increase your development of mindfulness. So, these non-meditative practices are really for everyone.

Much of what has been written about non-meditative approaches to shamatha is called *mindfulness in everyday life*. For example, Mirabai Bush discusses three non-meditative exercises that she calls *mindful reading*, *mindful writing*, and *mindful listening*. Mindful reading includes such practices as pausing to savor a particular phrase:

> Return to that phrase and repeat it to yourself, perhaps several times. Just sit with it. What does it evoke? Notice what images or ideas or memories arise. Do any of the words have meaning beyond the obvious? What meaning does this phrase give to the rest of what you're reading? Hold the phrase in your mind, giving it time to suggest more to you. Now reread the full piece. How is it different? Has your relationship to it changed? (Bush 2014, 73)

Mindful writing might include activities like pausing before pressing "Send" on an e-mail, visualizing the person who will receive it, anticipating what his or her reaction is likely to be, and then considering whether hitting "Send" is your most skillful option. Mindful listening involves making a conscious effort to be fully present when someone is speaking to us.

> [S]imply listen, without an agenda, to what is being said. If thoughts about other things arise, gently let them go and return to the speaker's words. As responses arise in your mind, wait until you've heard all that has to be said before replying. Try not to let your story overcome the speaker's. . . . Listen for feelings as well as the words. (Bush 2014, 76)

Bush's three mindful practices are an excellent way to begin a non-meditative approach to shamatha. But there are also other activities that you can incorporate into your daily life in order to increase the degree to which you remain aware of the present moment rather than getting caught up in regrets about the past or hopes and fears for the future.

For example, you can engage in *mindful action*. Choose an activity or chore that you usually perform mindlessly such as washing the dishes or vacuuming. The next time that you engage in it, rest your awareness on each aspect of the activity itself. Pay attention to every part of what you're doing and experiencing. Whenever your mind wanders, gently guide your attention back to the activity itself.

The technology that improves so much of modern life can hamper our attempts to be mindful. We're constantly having our attention distracted by incoming messages or e-mails, or we feel compelled to do an internet search to track down some random fact or other. ("Who was it that recorded 'Ferry Cross the Mersey' in the 1960s? Wait; let me check that on my phone.") But we can also co-opt our electronic devices to become tools for reinforcing our mindfulness.

To make your technology an ally rather than an impediment, set an alarm on your phone or computer to alert you on a regular basis, whatever works for you. In most cases, the shortest desirable cycle is every ten minutes (more frequently and the practice simply becomes a distraction), while the longest desirable cycle is an hour (less frequently and the practice doesn't occur often enough to make a difference). Then, whenever the alarm chimes, pay attention to that specific moment. What are you doing? What are you feeling? What is going on around you?

But mindfulness in everyday life can be "low tech" too. For example, you could place a sticky note somewhere where you'll encounter it occasionally throughout the day such as on the edge of your computer screen or the door of your office. The note could be blank, or you could write a short reminder to yourself such as "Be mindful" or "Experience this moment." Then, whenever you become aware of the sticky note, let your attention rest on what you're thinking, feeling, and experiencing at that specific moment.

At this point, someone might object: "You say that these practices are alternatives to meditation. But aren't they just different types of meditation? After all, you can meditate in lots of other ways than by sitting on a cushion (or even a chair) in a quiet room." There is some truth to this objection. It really depends on how broadly we wish to define the term *meditation*. And it's also true that certain activities people may not recognize as meditation really are meditation; they simply have misconceptions about what this practice actually involves.

There's a scene in the old NBC television show *Parks and Recreation* in which the park director Ron Swanson (played by Nick Offerman) believes that he has outsmarted the state auditor Chris Traeger (played by Rob Lowe), who insists that the office staff join him in meditating: "All told we were in there about six hours and no, I was not meditating. I just stood there quietly breathing. There were no thoughts in my head whatsoever. My mind was blank. I don't know what the hell these other crackpots were doing" (Ron Swanson Quotes 2014). We might quibble with the writer's assumption in this scene that meditation consists of having no thoughts in your head whatsoever, but the point is clear: Swanson was meditating even though he didn't realize it.

In a way, therefore, these suggested "non-meditative" practices really *are* a form of meditation. But because they don't involve the terminology and activities most people commonly associate with formal meditation, they're likely to be more palatable to some people than the shamatha technique described earlier.

THE OXYMORON OF AN EXPANDED FOCUS

Regardless of whether you pursue shamatha through formal meditation practice or these less formal, "non-meditative" practices, the goal is the same: to expand your focus on an awareness of the present moment. At first, of course, the phrase *expanded focus* seems like an oxymoron. Focus may seem, by its very nature to be clear, precise, and narrow. By broadening it, aren't you actually softening or blurring your focus, rather in the same way that softening your gaze while leaving your eyes open during meditation creates a more blurred field of vision?

What we need to realize, however, is that mental focus functions somewhat differently from visual focus. When we want to sharpen the focus with which we look at something, we train our field of vision exclusively on what we want to see more clearly. We ignore anything not directly related to what we're trying to see, at times even physically squinting so that we can narrow our gaze even further.

But as we saw in chapter 1, meditation (or, for that matter, mindfulness training in general) doesn't require hard concentration or *mental squinting*. To the contrary, as we gain greater mindfulness, we realize that most of the time we've been sampling only a fairly small part of our experience as it happens, "sipping life through a straw," as it were. But as we increase the degree to which we're aware of our experience, our attentiveness becomes broader and sharper simultaneously.

As academic leaders, we often give several workshops, lectures, and other presentations and have to become familiar with all kinds of video projectors and be adept at ways of connecting laptop computers to various kinds of media systems. On some projectors, the controls used to focus an image are separate from those used to zoom in or out of the image. As a result, if you broaden the image so that it fills the entire screen, the image becomes a blur, and you have to adjust an independent *focus ring* in order to restore clarity.

On more technically advanced projectors, focus and zoom can be linked. So, if you need to move the projector closer to the screen, you simply widen the zoom to fill the screen; if you need to move the projector farther toward the back of the room, you tighten the zoom so that the image doesn't extend beyond the screen. In either case, the projector maintains focus automatically: You don't have to worry about things becoming a blur simply because you've zoomed in or out depending on your current needs.

The first type of projector, for which zoom and focus are separate, is rather like how we traditionally approach the world: If we want to pay attention to one part of our experience, we have to readjust our focus. The second, more technologically advanced projector is a little like mindfulness: We can take in "the big picture" without losing our focus. When we're dealing with situations as complex and challenging as those involved in academic leadership, that combined broader and sharper focus is a strong asset.

FLOW

One other type of experience in which our frame of awareness traditionally tends to narrow (but this time in a wholly positive way) occurs in the state that the Hungarian psychologist Mihaly Csikszentmihalyi refers to as *flow*. Csikszentmihalyi defines flow as "the state in which people are so involved in an activity that nothing else seems to matter; the experience itself is so enjoyable that people will do it even at great cost, for the sheer sake of doing" (Csikszentmihalyi 1991, 4). We've all experienced a state like that, perhaps when we're engrossed in a good book or when we're engaged in some hobby that we care about deeply.

Flow often occurs when we're operating in the region that the Russian educational psychologist Lev Vygotsky called *the zone of proximal development*, that is to say when we're neither challenged so much that we become frustrated nor so little that we become bored (Vygotsky and Kozulin 1986, 187–89, and Vygotsky 1978, 86–89).

A number of authors have observed a similarity between flow and meditation, mindfulness, or both. To cite just a few examples,

- "Flow is a state of meditation—of mindfulness—that you're experiencing not while sitting quietly, but while fully and completely absorbed in an activity." (O'Brien 2014)
- "[M]editation will also increase your natural ability to achieve flow. Meditation lets you deliberately practice going into states of concentration, as well as filtering out distractions. A consistent meditation practice . . . will help you achieve flow much more consistently." (Axelsen 2015)
- "The flow state is like a moving meditation. Action and awareness merge when the athlete, artist or performer becomes totally absorbed in what they are doing. They have all the skills necessary and are able to stretch their abilities to meet the challenge, while focusing attention on the task at hand. Time seems to fly. It can also feel like there is no time." (Nemour 2013)
- "The Zone, or Flow, has been described in cultures around the world, but has a special connection to the Buddhist practice of mindfulness. Flow states can, and do, happen to us all the time, from playing music to sports or just a great conversation with friends or colleagues. But with mindfulness practice, one trains the mind to quiet the internal chatter that blocks Flow." (Whitaker 2016)

Certainly, one can see certain similarities between flow and mindfulness or meditation. Like mindfulness, flow is a pleasant and highly desirable state of mind that sometimes occurs spontaneously but that we can learn to enter more intentionally. Like meditation, flow gets easier and feels more natural the longer we engage in it.

But there's an important distinction between Csikszentmihalyi's original concept of flow and the type of mindfulness that we're pursuing in our efforts to become better academic leaders: Flow draws attention in to an activity; mindfulness increases our awareness, not just of all our activities, but of whatever's happening around us as well.

It's true, of course, that the type of meditation we're using as a means of improving mindfulness, single point meditation, does seek to rest our awareness, at least temporarily, on a specific subset of our experience. But remember: meditation is an exercise, a means to an end; it's not an end in itself. *Mindfulness* is the ultimate goal.

In that way, mindfulness and the type of flow we achieve through reading or other activities represent very different mental states. With flow, we focus on one activity and shut out the rest of the world; with mindfulness, we're as open to and aware of the rest of the world as possible. But what if there were a way to bring something of that spirit of flow to all of our activities and experiences? What if we could feel as attuned to everything we do in our work as we feel when our attention is completely engaged in baking or woodworking or riding horses or whatever activity we normally associate with flow?

That sensation is something that we might call *mindful flow*, and it represents a reasonable long-term goal for a mindfulness practice. It's the sort of achievement that doesn't come after only a year or two of mindful leadership, but it is possible, and it is worth pursuing. After engaging consistently in the mindful leadership practices that we'll explore in this book, you can find yourself at a point where the things that used to frustrate and annoy you seem less troubling and where the challenges that once seemed overwhelming appear like intriguing puzzles that would be pleasant to explore.

There are, unfortunately, only a few ways in which you can speed your progress toward mindful flow. But since these techniques are useful in the pursuit of mindfulness anyway, you might wish to include them in your practice.

- When you find that you're being annoyed or angered by what someone is doing, study that feeling instead of yielding to it. Think to yourself, "Remember: This is what being annoyed or angered feels like." Examine how the emotion makes you feel. Where is there tension in your body? What was the trigger that caused this emotion? Is your impulse about how to respond a skillful or an unskillful choice? We'll explore this process in much greater depth in chapter 5 where the practice known as cognitive diffusion is discussed.
- When you're feeling frustrated or having a bad day, ask yourself whether there are ways in which you can see humor in the situation. Occasionally,

even in the midst of an unpleasant event, someone might say, "This is going to make a funny story someday." Are there ways in which you can see your current situation as the basis for a funny story? How might that change in perspective make it easier to cope with the challenge?
- When confronted with a problem so overwhelming that you don't even know where to begin, imagine for a moment that the problem isn't happening to you but that you're reading about it as an interesting case study. If you were to advise some hypothetical academic leader about how to proceed in such a situation, what might you recommend? How, in other words, can you reinterpret the situation as an intriguing riddle rather than an overwhelming problem?
- When dealing with an incident that you're tempted to characterize as a crisis or disaster, ask yourself if you're still likely to feel that way one, five, or ten years from now. Is someone's life or health in jeopardy? Is the continued existence of the program or institution at risk? Is it possible that someone will lose his or her job? Is there a threat of significant loss of money involved? Will the resulting damage be irreparable? Could someone's reputation be ruined? If any of these possibilities exist, then you may indeed be facing a true crisis or disaster. If not, you may be overreacting to a situation that would be better addressed with a calmer, more systematic approach.
- When it seems as though your work is unfulfilling or that you're stuck in a grind, look for ways in which you can view what you're doing, not as a job or a career, but as a calling. The book *Positive Academic Leadership* traces the origins of the story, commonly retold in management books, about three men working on a construction site. Two of the workers are miserable, but the third seems to be enjoying the task. When asked what they're doing, the first two men speak only about the process they're engaged in: digging out dirt or earning a living. But the third worker says, "I'm building a cathedral!" (Buller 2013, 27). In many cases, seeing the purpose of what you're doing, not merely the process, can make your work more engaging. It's much more satisfying to see yourself as helping students achieve their life goals or promoting the discovery of important new ideas than completing assessment reports, balancing budgets, and attending seemingly endless meetings. (See also Lyubomirsky 2007, 188–89.)

In essence, what you are doing with each of these techniques is trying *intentionally* to capture some of the spirit of mindful flow that you hope someday will arise *naturally*. As with all aspects of mindfulness training, what's most required in order for these practices to work is patience. They will seem very artificial at first but grow easier and more productive over time.

WHAT SHAMATHA TEACHES US ABOUT ACADEMIC LEADERSHIP

Of course, our goal in this book is not merely to help you develop mindfulness—there are more than enough resources already available for that—but also to help you develop mindful academic leadership. So, it seems appropriate at this point to ask what shamatha teaches us about how we can be more effective as academic leaders.

Certain principles should be obvious by now. Being mindful as a leader means responding more intentionally to the situations that arise rather than reacting automatically. It means approaching each experience simply as an experience rather than as confirmation that someone we work with is "out to get us" or is trying to "ruin the program." It means keeping matters in perspective so that we're not operating in "crisis mode" all the time. But the implications of shamatha for academic leadership also go far beyond these obvious principles.

Let's consider three additional ways in which paying more attention to the present moment can help us become better academic leaders: reducing the likelihood of burnout for ourselves and others, diminishing the negative effect of our implicit biases, and conducting meetings that are more productive for everyone involved.

First, with regard to the question of burnout, we should start by realizing that this problem is severe and worsening. In a literature review, researchers Jenny Watts and Noelle Robertson at the University of Leicester found evidence that faculty burnout occurs at universities all over the world (Watts and Robertson 2011). Another study indicated that the cause of department chair burnout in one discipline was primarily due to the long hours demanded of academic leaders, the pressure of frequent budget cuts, interpersonal issues, and the emotional drain that occurs when faculty members had to be sanctioned or dismissed (Gabbe et al. 2002).

The pressures on faculty members, particularly early in their careers, to produce large amounts of research while still being innovative as teachers also creates burnout among the professoriate. Increasing demands to participate in student recruitment and retention, fundraising, assessment and accreditation activities, and strategic planning can produce a feeling of disconnect between what brought academics into the profession and what the job actually turned out to involve.

Not surprisingly, one study found that rates of burnout were particularly high among junior faculty members and far lower among those in more senior positions (Azeem and Nazir 2008). To some extent, that result is self-fulfilling: Highly exhausted and unfulfilled junior faculty members frequently leave the profession and never advance to the upper ranks.

But the pressures on untenured assistant professors (or on lecturers and readers in the system that Azeem and Nazir studied) are enormous. And it's not always easy for these junior faculty members to see the point of the various criteria by which they're being judged. There shouldn't be any cause for wonder, therefore, that many junior faculty members speak of the evaluation process at their institution as "jumping through hoops" rather than making genuine progress.

Moreover, the widespread use of performance-based funding systems and strategic planning in higher education causes both administrators and faculty members to engage in what seems like a never-ending process of setting and pursuing goals. There's rarely an opportunity to enjoy the attainment of any goal because new objectives must then be set, and the process of "continual improvement" never rests.

The shamatha approach to mindfulness—allowing one's attention to rest on the present moment—suggests possible solutions to these problems. For ourselves as academic leaders, periodic reminders to engage with what we're doing right now can provide a respite from the pressure we feel under to push toward the next goal, the improved performance metric, and the constant pressure we feel to live or die by the numbers. And if we give ourselves permission to take an occasional break from this drive toward whatever has been defined for us as more, higher, or better, we're likely to give our stressed faculty members permission to do so too.

One way in which we can help the faculty members in our areas avoid burnout and see the bigger picture of their accomplishments is simply to discuss with them the realities of professional burnout and demonstrate our awareness of this problem. Robert L. Minter, the former executive vice president and chief academic officer at Walsh College in Troy, Michigan, has developed an excellent seventy-question yes-or-no checklist faculty members can complete to help identify whether they are at risk of burnout and, if so, how severe the problem has become (Minter 2009). The questions on the checklist include such items as "You often display anger at those making demands of your time" and "You often feel that you've chosen the wrong profession."

By having faculty members complete Minter's checklist during a retreat or extended meeting and then pointing out resources available to them for coping with work-related stress such as the opportunities that might be included in an Employee Assistance Program, we can go a long way toward improving faculty morale—which often translates into improved student learning (Furrer, Skinner, and Pitzer 2014, and Brandi, Alan, and Marjorie 2015)—at the same time that we reduce costs through lower faculty turnover.

Studies performed by Sonja Lyubomirsky also provide what almost becomes a formula for increasing our own job satisfaction and performance as academic leaders by broadening our focus on the present moment. Lyubomirsky conducted research on various groups that were assigned specific tasks to perform at specific intervals and found that the following strategies had the most significant and lasting impact on the participant's overall sense of well-being:

- *Taking time once a week to write down three to five things for which the participant was grateful.* In an academic setting, this practice might consist of starting or ending the workweek by recording "Three good things that happened during the past week" or "Five good things my colleagues did recently." Engaging in this practice more often than once a week simply made Lyubomirsky's test subjects see the activity as one more chore they had to do. Performing the activity less often than once a week made it too infrequent to have a real impact. (Lyubomirsky 2007, 96, 128)
- *Choosing one day a week to perform either one large act of kindness or three to five minor acts of kindness beyond those which they would ordinarily have done.* We all have our own habits and patterns of kindness. Some people do favors for others, write notes of encouragement or gratitude, and allow other cars to pull in front of them in busy parking garages multiple times every day. Others do so only rarely when they're in a particularly good mood. The key to this strategy is simply to increase whatever rate is natural for you by one major act of kindness (such as offering to babysit for a beleaguered parent) or three to five small acts (like stopping by someone's office to thank the person for an insightful observation at a faculty meeting) per week. In other words, do something nice beyond what you'd ordinarily do. Lyubomirsky's research demonstrated that this strategy improved the participant's sense of happiness (and likely had a similar effect on those who benefitted from the person's added generosity). (Lyubomirsky 2007, 133)
- *Spending a few seconds each day to savor an ordinary experience the participant would ordinarily have rushed through.* Lyubomirsky cites experiments conducted by Martin Seligman, Tayyab Rashid, Acacia Parks, and Stephen Schueller in which participants were encouraged to relish fairly routine and ordinary experiences (Seligman, Rashid, and Parks 2006; Schueller 2006). "In all these studies those participants prompted to practice [the activity of] savoring [ordinary experiences] regularly showed significant increases in happiness and reductions in depression" (Lyubomirsky 2007, 194). It may be one thing to accept intellectually that there's benefit in learning how to "stop and smell the roses," but the research demonstrates that actually engaging in this strategy causes one to have a more positive outlook on one's life or work.

Lyubomirsky cautions that living *constantly* in the present can be too much of a good thing (Lyubomirsky 2007, 204). Reflecting on the past allows us to draw lessons from it, and planning for the future allows us to be prepared to take advantage of opportunities when they arise.

But if we remember that mindful academic leadership doesn't *force* us to think only of the present moment, but *allows* us to switch more intentionally back and forth between autopilot and mindfulness, we recognize that shamatha exercises give us one more tool for our leadership toolkit: an ability to be more nonjudgmentally aware of what's happening to us and around us whenever we need to be.

IMPLICIT BIAS

The second leadership advantage that shamatha conveys is the improved ability to compensate for our own implicit biases, our unconscious tendency to prejudge people and situations. A great deal of recent research has shown that, no matter how free we think we may be of biases and thinking in stereotypes, such factors color our decision making. In fact, our choices are frequently determined by bias milliseconds before our rational decision-making processes even begin.

Project Implicit, operated out of Harvard University but developed in conjunction with several other universities, offers a series of online tests that evaluates the speed and accuracy with which participants respond to a number of questions that deal with race, gender, age, skin tone, whether the subject is holding a weapon or a harmless object, religion, sexual orientation, and many other ways in which people characterize other people and interpret their actions (Project Implicit 2011).

What these tests repeatedly indicate is that "[t]he implicit associations we hold *do not necessarily align with our declared beliefs* or even reflect stances we would explicitly endorse" (The Ohio State University 2015; emphasis in original). In other words, even though we might find it horrifying that a person would judge others on such factors as race, gender, or ethnicity, we all tend to do it.

In fact, implicit biases affect our decisions so quickly and at such a subconscious level that we're not even aware they influenced us. The reasons we give for making our decisions are thus developed only later, after our emotions had already decided the matter "for us." In addition, people tend to incorporate new information very quickly into their current belief systems, *even if that information might appear to contradict or disprove those systems* (Smith, Ratliff, and Nosek 2012).

One major study of doctors revealed that, although the participants exhibited no racial bias they were aware of, they nevertheless prescribed treatments in a racially biased manner (Green et al. 2007). Another study indicated that this tendency increased as emergency departments became more overcrowded and the physicians were forced to deal with more patients simultaneously (Johnson et al. 2016).

It would not be surprising, therefore, if the decisions of academic leaders were also affected by their own implicit biases—even biases that they'd vehemently deny they had if asked—and that this effect would increase as we had to deal with more stakeholders or make more decisions under greater time pressure. By developing our ability to switch between heuristics and mindful decision making more intentionally, we may thus be able to reduce the negative effects of implicit bias and select options that more completely reflect the values we believe in.

Awareness of the present moment alerts us to the possibility that we may be making a decision at a time when we're tired, under stress, anxious about something unrelated to the decision itself, feeling rushed, or depleted due to all the other decisions we had to make that day. Shamatha mindfulness can return our attention to more objective criteria for making the decision and increase the likelihood that we'll proceed in a way that best reflects our core values.

MEETING MINDFULLY WITH SHAMATHA

Perhaps the most obvious task in which we engage without mindful engagement is attending or conducting meetings. We typically hold meetings, not because anything significant needs to be addressed by the group, but because there's a meeting scheduled or we think that "we really ought to meet" to discuss some issue. But without a compelling reason for being there, members of the group begin to "check out" mentally, we find the same points being raised over and over, and virtually no one leaves the meeting feeling that his or her time has been well spent there.

Mindful academic leaders reverse this trend by conducting meetings that are organized effectively, focused on important issues, and interesting. By being fully aware of each moment, they don't lose sight of how precious and fleeting each moment is. Have you ever been in a meeting where you were thinking, "Isn't the person who organized this aware of what a waste of time this is? Doesn't he or she know or care that we have better things to do?"

Mindful academic leaders don't make the mistake of assuming that people have unlimited time available or that what's important to them must be equally important to everyone else. They're aware that, whenever people are at meetings, they're not conducting research, working on their courses, or implementing the decisions that came out of their *last* meetings. For this reason, they meet only when getting together in person is the best way of dealing with a matter, and even then they take care to be respectful of the investment of time that others are making.

Meeting mindfully also occurs when the person in charge takes steps to direct the attention of everyone present to the most important issues. One way of achieving this goal is phrasing agenda items as questions to be answered or problems to be solved. For instance, at a curriculum meeting, a heading like New Course Proposals actually doesn't provide the members of the group with very much direction. As a result, discussions can easily get off track.

If, however, that section of the agenda were headed "Should the Following Course Proposals Be Approved as They Are, Amended, or Rejected?" that very question helps focus the discussion. In addition, if the discussion does become unfocused, restoring people's attention to the key issue is a simple matter of gently reminding them of the question specified on the agenda. Your task as meeting leader is then very similar to what you do when you realize that your thoughts have wandered off during shamatha meditation: You kindly and respectfully guide the focus back to the task at hand.

Another way of helping meetings become more mindful is to agree that the time spent together will be as interruption-free as possible. It's counterproductive to require people to turn their electronic devices off or to leave them at the door—many people use their phones, laptops, and tablets to take notes these days—but it's a reasonable request to ask people to silence their devices so that they don't disturb the flow of the meeting.

Leaders can seem unreasonable if they demand that those in attendance never check their texts or e-mails during the meeting. They can, however, politely ask that people devote most of their attention to the meeting itself, looking at texts and e-mails discreetly and only occasionally. Moreover, if the meeting is well-constructed with significant issues that those attending will care about, people will be less tempted by these distractions.

We'll discover other ways of meeting mindfully in the chapters that follow since different approaches to mindfulness have their own contributions to make to effective meetings. For the moment, however, if you have a particular interest in the concept of mindful meetings, good resources to examine include Pavlov and Tobias (2014) and Williams (2015).

KEY POINTS FROM CHAPTER 2

- Regular practice is more important than the length of individual meditation sessions in cultivating mindfulness.
- Despite what many meditation instructors may tell you, specific postures and hand positions are irrelevant to the quality of your meditation in a

secular practice. The only important factor with regard to posture is to choose a comfortable position in which you'll remain alert.
- Shamatha meditation is a technique for increasing mindfulness by practicing repeated awareness of the breath.
- Various practices that are commonly referred to as *mindfulness in everyday life* provide a non-meditative path to the advantages of shamatha.
- There are ways in which the non-meditative approaches to shamatha *are* actually a form of meditation. They just don't involve the sitting or walking practices commonly associated with traditional meditation.
- Mindfulness creates our ability to have an expanded focus, an awareness of what is happening to us and around us that is simultaneously clearer and broader than the way in which we habitually take in our experiences.
- Although flow, the state in which we become so engaged in an activity that nothing else seems to matter, is sometimes associated with meditation or mindfulness, it is actually quite different. Flow eliminates distractions; meditation and mindfulness help us to see through distractions, to regard them as simply part of a larger, more comprehensive experience.
- We might call the ability to become actively and fully engaged with the entirety of our experience *mindful flow*, and that ability develops for most people only after a prolonged meditation practice or devotion to non-meditative alternatives.
- Shamatha mindfulness improves our effectiveness as academic leaders because it helps us avoid burnout (and places us in a better position to prevent burnout in others), reduces the negative impact of our implicit biases, and offers us a strategy for conducting meetings in a more mindful and productive manner.

EXERCISES TO COMPLETE BEFORE PROCEEDING TO CHAPTER 3

1. If you find yourself getting bored by the shamatha meditation technique described in this chapter, you can vary it a bit by trying one or more of the following alterations:
    - Experiment with different ways of resting your gaze. If you have been meditating with your eyes closed, open them or vice versa. When your eyes are open, experiment with different ways of resetting the soft focus of your eyes such as by setting your gaze on the floor immediately in front of you, six to ten feet out, straight in front of you, and so on.
    - Practice *walking meditation*: Walk slowly in some quiet area. Rest your attention on the heel, sole, and ball of each foot as it makes contact with the ground and comes up again.

- Practice *massage meditation*: Schedule a massage with a professional masseuse and then, during the massage, simply let your attention rest on wherever the masseuse's fingers and hands come into contact with your body.
2. The next time that something unpleasant happens—you stub your toe, someone unloads his or her anger on you unfairly, you find yourself filled with self-doubt, and so on—don't give in to those negative feelings, but consciously, intentionally make your mind approach them with curiosity. Rest your awareness on those feelings in much the same way that you rest your attention on the breath during shamatha meditation. See if this activity causes you to respond more skillfully than you would have done before. (Keep in mind that your most skillful response might be a strategic lack of response.)
3. If you've chosen to pursue shamatha with a non-meditative strategy, see if you can develop your own set of techniques for periodically reminding yourself to be aware of the present moment. Some people play drinking games where they down a drink every time a politician uses a certain phrase in a speech or when a stock joke is made yet again in a sitcom. Perhaps you can transform this practice into a healthier and more life-affirming awareness game: Every time your boss uses one of his or her pet phrases or every time a student asks you whether you did anything important in a class that he or she missed, don't get angry; instead, try to become aware of everything you can about that moment. Try to notice your feelings, the other person's facial expressions, the temperature in the room, and whatever else you can.

REFERENCES

Axelsen, R. 2015. "Flow and Meditation." *Daily Meditate*, March 23, 2015. Retrieved from http://dailymeditate.com/flow-and-meditation/.

Azeem, S. M., and N. A. Nazir. 2008. "A Study of Job Burnout among University Teachers." *Psychology and Developing Societies* 20 (1): 51–64.

Brandi, N. F., K. G. Alan, and M. B. Marjorie. 2015. "Students' Instructional Dissent and Relationships with Faculty Members' Burnout, Commitment, Satisfaction, and Efficacy." *Communication Education* 64 (1): 65–82.

Buller, J. L. 2013. *Positive Academic Leadership: How to Stop Putting Out Fires and Start Making a Difference*. San Francisco, CA: Jossey-Bass.

Bush, M. 2014. "A Higher Education." *Mindful* 2, no. 1 (April): 70–76.

Chödrön, P. 2005. *When Things Fall Apart: Heart Advice for Difficult Times*. Boston: Shambhala.

Csikszentmihalyi, M. 1991. *Flow: The Psychology of Optimal Experience*. New York: Harper Perennial.

Davich, V. N. 2014. *8 Minute Meditation: Quiet Your Mind, Change Your Life* (2nd ed.). New York: Perigee.
Furrer, C. J., E. A. Skinner, and J. R. Pitzer. 2014. "The Influence of Teacher and Peer Relationships on Students' Classroom Engagement and Everyday Motivational Resilience." *Teachers College Record* 116 (13): 101–23.
Gabbe, S. G., J. Melville, L. Mandel, and E. Walker. 2002. "Burnout in Chairs of Obstetrics and Gynecology: Diagnosis, Treatment, and Prevention." *American Journal of Obstetrics and Gynecology* 186 (4): 601–12.
Green, A. R., D. R. Carney, D. J. Pallin, L. H. Ngo, K. L. Raymond, L. I. Iezzoni, and M. R. Banaji. 2007. "Implicit Bias among Physicians and Its Prediction of Thrombolysis Decisions for Black and White Patients." *Journal of General Internal Medicine* 22, no. 9 (August 10): 1231–38.
Johnson, T. J., R. W. Hickey, G. E. Switzer, E. Miller, D. G. Winger, M. Nguyen, R. A. Saladino, and L. R. Hausmann. 2016. "The Impact of Cognitive Stressors in the Emergency Department on Physician Implicit Racial Bias." *Academic Emergency Medicine: Official Journal of the Society for Academic Emergency Medicine* 23 (3): 297–305.
Lyubomirsky, S. 2007. *The How of Happiness: A Practical Guide to Getting the Life You Want.* New York: Penguin.
Michie, D. 2014. *Mindfulness Is Better Than Chocolate.* New York: The Experiment/Mosaic Reputation Management.
Minter, R. L. 2009. "Faculty Burnout." *Contemporary Issues in Education Research* 2 (2): 1–8.
Nemour, S. 2013. "The Zone: Use Breath, Posture and Passion to Get into the Flow State." *Huffington Post*, October 29, 2013. Retrieved from http://www.huffingtonpost.com/stacey-nemour/meditation-practice_b_4133875.html.
O'Brien, M. 2014. "How to Enter the 'Flow State' Any Time: 4 Simple Steps." *Melli O'Brien*. Retrieved from https://mrsmindfulness.com/how-you-can-enter-mindfulness-in-4-simple-steps/.
Pavlov, A., and J. Tobias. 2014. "Mindful Meetings." *Management Focus*, May 15, 2014. Retrieved from http://www.som.cranfield.ac.uk/som/dinamic-content/media/Sherry%20Davison/management_focus_issue_36_mindful_meetings.pdf.
Project Implicit. 2011. "Preliminary Information." Retrieved from https://implicit.harvard.edu/implicit/takeatest.html.
Ron Swanson Quotes. 2014 (September 11). "Ep. 19: Live Ammo: Mind Was Blank." Retrieved from http://swansonquotes.com/quotes/season04/ep-19-live-ammo-mind-blank/#.WTgRD7GZO3I.
Schueller, S. M. 2006. "Personality Fit and Positive Interventions." Unpublished manuscript. Philadelphia: Department of Psychology, University of Pennsylvania.
Seligman, M. E. P., T. Rashid, and A. C. Parks. 2006. "Positive Psychotherapy." *American Psychologist* 61 (8): 774–88.
Smith, C. T., K. A. Ratliff, and B. A. Nosek. 2012. "Rapid Assimilation: Automatically Integrating New Information with Existing Beliefs." *Social Cognition* 30, no. 2 (April): 199–219.

The Ohio State University. 2015. "Understanding Implicit Bias." Retrieved from http://kirwaninstitute.osu.edu/research/understanding-implicit-bias/.
Vygotsky, L. S. 1978. "Interaction between Learning and Development." Translated by M. Lopez-Morillas. In *Mind in Society: The Development of Higher Psychological Processes*, edited by M. Cole, V. John-Steiner, S. Scribner, and E. Souberman, 79–91. Cambridge, MA: Harvard.
Vygotsky, L. S., and A. Kozulin (Eds.). 1986. *Thought and Language*. Revised. Cambridge, MA: MIT Press.
Watts, J., and N. Robertson. 2011. "Burnout in University Teaching Staff: A Systematic Literature Review." *Educational Research* 53, no. 1 (March): 33–50.
Whitaker, J. 2016. "7 Characteristics of Flow States and How Mindfulness Brings Us There." *Patheos*, August 8, 2016. Retrieved from http://www.patheos.com/blogs/americanbuddhist/2016/08/7-characteristics-of-flow-states-how-mindfulness-brings-us-there.html.
Williams, R. 2015. "How to Bring Mindfulness into Meetings—10 Tips." *Psychology Today*. Retrieved from https://www.psychologytoday.com/blog/wired-success/201510/how-bring-mindfulness-meetings-10-tips.
Yackle, K., L. A. Schwarz, K. Kam, J. M. Sorokin, J. R. Huguenard, J. L. Feldman, L. Luo, and M. A. Krasnow. 2017. "Breathing Control Center Neurons That Promote Arousal in Mice." *Science* 355, no. 6332 (March 30): 1411–15.

RESOURCES

Lamrimpa, G., B. A. Wallace, and H. Sprager. 2011. *How to Practice Shamatha Meditation: The Cultivation of Meditative Quiescence*. Ithaca, NY: Snow Lion.
Rosenberg, L. 2004. *Breath by Breath: The Liberating Practice of Insight Liberation*. Boston: Shambhala.
Stahl, B., and E. Goldstein. 2010. *A Mindfulness-Based Stress Reduction Workbook*. Oakland, CA: New Harbinger Publications.
Wallace, B. A. 2007. *The Attention Revolution: Unlocking the Power of the Focused Mind*. Boston: Wisdom Publications.
Waning, A. 2014. *"The Less Dust, the More Trust": Participating in the Shamatha Project, Meditation and Science*. Winchester, UK: Mantra.

Chapter 3

Vipassana

Expanding Clarity

If the goal of shamatha was to expand our awareness of the present moment, the next approach to mindfulness that we'll take involves expanding awareness of our *experience* during each passing moment. The distinction is subtle but important.

When we're paying attention to the present moment, we're less likely to be distracted by our regrets about the past, those "might have been thoughts" or those pangs of "could've, would've, should've" that keep us from taking full advantage of opportunities before us right now. We also don't get caught up in worrying about the future so much that we forget to take the steps in the present that would make that more desirable future possible.

Being aware of our experience of the present moment adds a further dimension to this level of mindfulness. We become more conscious of the feelings that we undergo and are thus better able to interpret those experiences as nothing more than feelings, if that's a more skillful response.

An example may help to illustrate the importance of this concept. Have you ever been so angry or so upset that you said something you later wish you hadn't? (Of course, you have. Everyone has.) Imagine that, at the moment of that experience, you could expand your mental clarity so that it occurred to you to think, "Oh, this is merely anger. It will go away before too long," or, "I can sense that I'm upset right now. I should wait to respond until I've calmed down."

This greater mindfulness of experience is sometimes called *vipassana* (pronounced vih-PAH-shyuh-nuh or vih-PAHS-suh-nuh), a Pali word meaning insight, seeing clearly, or seeing things as they really are. (Sanskrit and

Pali are both Indian languages, and they're closely related. While purists will object to this simplification, unless you're a linguist, you can think of the relationship between Sankrit and Pali as a little bit like the relationship between Latin and Italian.) For this reason, vipassana meditation is sometimes known in English as *insight meditation*. Like shamatha meditation, it's another exercise in resting one's awareness on a single point. This time, however, the single point of awareness is your experience, not your breath.

S. N. GOENKA

Perhaps the figure who did the most to increase global familiarity with vipassana was S. N. Goenka (1924–2013), an industrialist from Myanmar who first began to study meditation because he hoped it would relieve the severity of his migraines. Finding the vipassana approach to meditation to be a life-transforming experience, Goenka left his business in the care of his family, moved to India, and became a teacher.

Goenka's approach, which remained almost unchanged throughout his career, was to conduct ten-day retreats without charge, not even for food or lodging. His centers were supported solely by the voluntary contributions of those who had completed his program and received benefit from it. The first four days are devoted to practice in meditation on the breath, which is very similar to the shamatha technique that we explored in chapter 2. The idea is that this type of meditation provides the appropriate level of calm that allows the vipassana technique to achieve its greatest effect.

The remainder of the ten-day retreat is spent learning about and practicing the vipassana technique itself, which is explained later in this chapter. In order to maintain consistent instruction among his worldwide centers, Goenka's own recordings are used as the primary means of construction. Although Goenka insisted that his approach to vipassana had a thoroughly scientific basis, several of his views—such as his belief that mind was not merely a function of the brain but was also present throughout the entire body (Hart 1987, 29) and that sexual relations between any two consenting adults are not permissible (Hart 1987, 64–65)—seem alien, even demonstrably wrong to many Western readers.

For this reason, the vipassana technique that we'll explore in this book will be modified somewhat from that used in Goenka's retreat centers and detached from its Buddhist framework. Our goal, after all, is to develop greater mindfulness as academic leaders, not to master the ideology of any particular philosophical or religious system.

VIPASSANA MEDITATION

For the method of vipassana meditation that we'll use, these are the steps that you'll follow:

1. Complete the standard meditation preparation as described in chapter 2.
2. Pause for a moment to set aside your normal work and activities, focusing your attention on the fact that you're about to meditate. If it helps to do so, practice the shamatha technique for several breaths until you feel calm and prepared to begin the exercise.
3. Set a timer for five minutes.
4. Mentally scan the sensory impressions you feel in each part of your body, starting from your toes and moving up.
5. Notice each impression, but don't judge it or dwell on it. Label the impression using one of the words in table 3.1 or a similar, objective, non-emotional term.
6. After noting each sensation for a moment, let it go, and proceed to the next sensation.
7. If you sense pain, notice it, but don't fixate on it. Pay attention to it for a moment, and then move on.
8. Do the same thing for other sensations that you'd typically find unpleasant. For example, if a part of your body itches, don't scratch it. Simply label it *itching* and then notice the next sensory impression.
9. Move at your own pace. If you reach the top of your head, then start moving back down.
10. From time to time you may realize that your attention has wandered off and you've been thinking of things other than the meditation. Whenever this occurs, simply guide your attention gently back to the last part of your body you recall scanning. (If you don't remember where you left off, start over anywhere.) As we saw with shamatha meditation, having to guide your mind back after it has become distracted doesn't mean that you've failed at the meditation. Guiding your mind back *is* the meditation.
11. Continue this process until the timer goes off.

Table 3.1 Objective, Non-emotional Terms

hearing	tasting	tightness
seeing	thinking	looseness
smelling	pressure	warmth
coolness	tension	darkness
tingling	loosening	change
numbness	brightness	continuing

For a more thorough discussion of the traditional vipassana technique of meditation as taught by Goenka, see Glickman 2002, 92–100.

As you continue your practice of vipassana meditation, you're likely to notice two things occurring. First, you'll observe more and more sensations the more frequently you practice this technique. Initially your body scan may be quite superficial. You'll be aware of a bit of pressure in this or that body part, hear a few sounds in the background, and become aware of how the light flickers in the room.

But after engaging in this practice for several weeks, you're likely to notice that the environment around us is a far more complex and nuanced place than we typically recognize. We do so many things on autopilot that it becomes second nature to screen out the rich sensations of our environment. As we become more mindful, our ability to "raise" and "lower" those screens at will becomes more advanced.

Second, you'll probably find it easier over time to deal with unpleasant sensations as they occur. One of the advantages that vipassana meditation brings is practice in noticing sensations (regardless of whether they're good, bad, or indifferent), paying attention to them, but then realizing that they're only sense impressions.

That's a desirable skill to have when your arm's in a cast, your elbow is itching, and you can't do anything about it. It's also desirable when that person who always annoys you starts "pressing your buttons" again. You have the option of thinking "Oh, my elbow is itching" or "That person is saying those irritating things again" but not reacting if that would be a more skillful choice for you.

If one of the benefits of shamatha meditation is understanding—not just intellectually, but also completely and intuitively—that each moment is fleeting and should be seen for nothing more or less than what it is, then vipassana meditation deepens that understanding. It causes us to realize that our feelings and sense impressions are *only* feelings and sense impressions. Like fleeting moments, they also tend to pass, and we don't have to respond to every one of them.

Vipassana meditation thus increases our options. The next time we're in a meeting and we feel angry, we can explore that feeling and simply "be" with it for a moment or two before deciding on our most skillful response. If the anger stems from righteous indignation over a genuine wrong that's being done to people who can't defend themselves, then our best option might be to intervene and to do so aggressively. But if the anger stems from something foolish that someone said carelessly or thoughtlessly, our best option might not be to react right then; it may even be not to react at all. Vipassana meditation gives us greater control over an emotional "switch" that we may once have thought was completely beyond our control.

NON-MEDITATIVE APPROACHES TO VIPASSANA

As valuable as vipassana meditation can be, however, there are non-meditative strategies that we can use to achieve the same goals, just as we did when we were exploring shamatha. The non-meditative approaches to vipassana are of two primary types: *strategies for greater self-awareness* and *strategies for greater awareness of our experience*. We'll explore each of these individually, beginning with ways in which each of us can become more self-aware.

Chade-Meng Tan is a former software engineer who provided workshops at Google shaped by Jon Kabat-Zinn's Mindfulness-Based Stress Reduction system. Over time, Tan developed more and more of his own approaches to mindfulness, many of which stem from the notion that happiness is a state of mind that can be increased through greater self-awareness.

In his book, *Search Inside Yourself*, Tan defines self-awareness as "knowledge of one's internal states, preferences, resources, and intuitions" (Tan 2012, 11). The overall goal of this self-awareness is to make sure that your actions are properly aligned with your core values, purposes, and priorities. The idea is this: If what you do flows directly from who you are as a person and what you care most deeply about, you're less likely to choose unskillful options and thus regret your actions later.

Tan recommends a number of non-meditative techniques people can use to increase their self-awareness. One exercise that can be particularly effective is journaling, with the intent of self-discovery. Tan recommends developing a number of prompts, writing each on a separate piece of paper, and drawing a prompt at random each day to kick-start a few minutes of free-thought journaling. The prompts that Tan recommends are as follows:

What I am feeling now is . . .
I am aware that . . .
What motivates me is . . .
I am inspired by . . .
Today, I aspire to . . .
What hurts me is . . .
I wish . . .
Others are . . .
I made a happy mistake . . .
Love is . . .
(Tan 2012, 97)

Here are some additional prompts that you may wish to consider:

At this very moment, the thing that I'm proudest of is . . .
My greatest hope for today is . . .
I find that I become annoyed when . . .
The core value that seems most important to me today is . . .
The last time I was angry was when . . .
My biggest fear is . . .
The one word I'd use to describe myself today is . . .
If I could have my wish, I'd love for someone to come up to me and say . . .
The biggest regret I have is . . .
My best days at work occur when . . .

After working with these prompts for a few weeks, you'll undoubtedly develop a few of your own. It's best to have a large enough set to work from that you truly can't predict which prompt you're likely to draw that day. At the same time, you don't want to have so large a set of prompts that you never draw the same one twice. It can be a useful practice of self-awareness to compare how you finished a sentence like "My greatest hope for today is . . ." on two occasions several months apart. What was different about what you were experiencing on those two dates that made your responses different too?

Another non-meditative exercise that Tan recommends is writing your own obituary. What do you hope that people will say about you after you've died? What would you like your legacy to be? Are you currently making choices that will cause that legacy to be likely? Tan even recommends writing two different forms of your obituary: one by extrapolating from the path that you're on right now and one reflecting the life that you aspire to live. What would you have to do differently in order to make the path you're on right now lead you toward the life you aspire to have? Are you even on the right path? (Tan 2012, 142).

If journaling and writing obituaries don't appeal to you, another way of achieving a higher degree of self-awareness is to complete the various inventories that are available through the University of Pennsylvania's Authentic Happiness Questionnaire Center (University of Pennsylvania 2017). The great advantage of the University of Pennsylvania program over similar websites is that all the inventories that it provides have been extensively validated. In other words, what they reveal about your personality is actually based on extensive research and verified through numerous tests; it isn't just someone's opinion.

For the purpose of increasing self-awareness, you may wish to explore the following inventories from the University of Pennsylvania's Authentic Happiness Questionnaire Center:

- The Authentic Happiness Inventory
- The Optimism Test

- The Gratitude Survey
- The Grit (i.e., perseverance) Survey
- The Work-Life [Satisfaction] Questionnaire
- The Satisfaction with Life Scale
- The Meaning in Life Questionnaire

These inventories can reveal aspects of your personality that you've never really thought about or that you've found it difficult to admit to yourself. For example, the VIA [Values in Action] Strength Survey is an instrument that has you respond to a comprehensive set of statements and then ranks the degree to which you adhere to twenty-four principles, values, or what the survey itself calls "character strengths."

For example, when I completed this inventory, the results ranked the five values or principles that were most important to me in the following order:

1. Love of learning
2. Curiosity and interest in the world
3. Judgment, critical thinking, and open-mindedness
4. Humor and playfulness
5. Hope, optimism, and future-mindedness

I didn't find these results particularly surprising, and no one who knows me at all well would be surprised by them either.

The truly interesting results came when the inventory calculated the five principles or values that were *least* important to me.

20. Modesty and humility
21. Bravery and valor
22. Citizenship, teamwork, and loyalty
23. Kindness and generosity
24. Spirituality, sense of purpose, and faith

Okay, there have been times when my sense of accomplishment probably did outweigh my humility, and I've always been the sort of person who regards intellect and skepticism as far more important than spirituality and faith. I'll even admit to not always being the bravest person in the room.

But kindness, teamwork, and citizenship? Those were always qualities that I tried hard to exemplify in both my personal and professional lives. Could a thoroughly validated inventory really suggest that these qualities weren't important to me?

As I studied the entire ranking of the twenty-four items on the VIA strengths list, it gradually became apparent that the inventory had revealed certain tendencies in myself that I had been reluctant to acknowledge.

When push came to shove and I had to choose between generosity and, say, critical thinking, it was indeed true that critical thinking was likely to win out. The same thing was true if I had to make a choice between "industry, diligence, and perseverance" (my tenth-ranked value) and citizenship, teamwork, and loyalty (twenty-second on my list). The more I gave careful consideration to the results of the inventory, in other words, the more I could see that they were an accurate reflection of the values that truly informed my actions and decisions, not merely the values that, to flatter myself, I wanted to *think* I supported.

In many ways, that's the purpose of the VIA Strengths Inventory. All twenty-four of the strengths explored represent positive qualities. And although anyone who looks at the list might find two or three of them and conclude, "I really don't care about that value very much," there will still remain at least twenty on the list that the person will care about and truly believe are guiding principles for his or her actions.

The self-awareness aspect of the inventory comes in seeing how the choices we make while taking the survey shape the priority order of our strengths and values when we see the results. The top five values probably won't surprise us, but the bottom five or ten might. "Do I really care so little about that?" we may think when the results appear. If we're candid in our self-analysis, the answer is likely to be that, in terms of how we act in real-world situations, we don't care as much about some moral principles as we think we do.

THE SELF-AWARENESS SELFIE

Another useful exercise to increase our self-awareness in a non-meditative fashion is to take what we might call a *Self-Awareness Selfie*. To engage in this exercise, you simply take four sheets of paper and write as many words as possible in response to each of the following prompts.

On the first piece of paper, write down every *noun* you can think of that applies to you. The nouns you come up with may include professional words (*professor, department chair, dean*, and the like), relationship words (*son* or *daughter, husband* or *wife, father* or *mother*, and the like), and anything else that comes to mind (*citizen of* some specific country, *optimist* or *pessimist, member of* some specific organization, and the like).

On the second piece of paper, write down every *adjective* you can think of that applies to you. Are you more generous or self-interested? Introverted or extroverted? Cautious or daring? Humorous or serious? Don't be limited by just these few examples; try to think of all the terms that you or those who know you would use to describe you.

On the third piece of paper, write down as many things you can think of that you believe are true but cannot prove. That title, *What We Believe but Cannot Prove*, is actually used for a collection of short essays contributed by scientists and other scholars to *The Edge* website (www.edge.org) and edited by the author and literary agent John Brockman (Brockman 2006). The idea is that even the most data-obsessed, empirically minded among us make an occasional leap of faith. It may not be as great a leap as a belief in intelligent life on other planets or the ability of the dead to communicate with the living, but there are certain unprovable convictions in everyone's worldview. Which of your convictions haven't yet been validated by evidence and may not even be verifiable?

On the last piece of paper, write down the virtues, values, or principles that you believe in the most. What are the ideals that most guide your actions? And what are the ideals that you wish would guide your actions more frequently? List these values just as you did the words on the other three pieces of paper. As you conduct this exercise, feel free to go back and forth among the different parts. For example, thinking of a value that you admire might cause you to think of a good adjective you could use to describe yourself or vice versa. Keep filling up your four pieces of paper until you can't think of anything more to say.

Once you complete the writing part of this exercise, the editing part begins. For each of your four lists, sort the words and phrases you've written into priority order. In other words, of all the nouns you've listed to describe yourself, which nouns describe you the best? Which of these nouns, if you were to eliminate them from your list, would cause this catalog of who you are and what you believe in to lack something essential?

Conversely, are there words and phrases that now look extraneous? Do you find yourself thinking thoughts like, "Well, I wrote down here that I'm a member of the Suffolk Tennis Club. But I was thinking of letting that membership expire anyway. I hardly go, and that really doesn't define who I am"? If so, feel free to delete those extraneous items from your lists.

When you're finished, look at the highest priority items on each of the lists. Do they capture the "real you"? Would someone who knows you best—and who may even be more objective about you than you are—recognize you from those lists? If so, then you've created a true Self-Awareness Selfie. Using the information provided on your lists, write a one-paragraph candid profile of yourself. Don't look only at the façade that you project to the rest of the world, but try to capture your own, true, authentic self.

If you don't believe that the information recorded on your lists reflects the "real you," go back and keep working at this exercise until you can honestly say that you've successfully captured the essence of who you are. Don't worry: No one is going to see the results of this exercise unless you decide to share them. Our purpose at the moment is simply to provide you with a clearer image of your identity and values as a means of helping you become a more effective academic leader.

HOW DOES GREATER SELF-AWARENESS IMPROVE OUR LEADERSHIP?

That last sentence, however, raises important questions: Does greater self-awareness actually make us better academic leaders and, if so, how? In an article appearing in the *Harvard Business Review*, Susan David and Christine Congleton discuss a concept that they call *emotional agility* that, they believe, allows people to approach the emotional experiences that are likely to arise in the workplace using a mindful, values-driven, and productive approach rather than simply feeding those emotions or trying to suppress them (David and Congleton 2013).

They recommend four steps to improve a person's emotional agility, each of which bears a significant relationship to the type of self-awareness we've just been exploring:

Step One: Recognize Your Patterns

Pay attention to when you're using heuristics rather than observation and reason in your decision-making processes. As we've seen, using heuristics is not necessarily a bad thing, but it's important for us to be aware when we're doing so. The more readily we can recognize when we're acting mindlessly and on autopilot, the more readily we can catch ourselves before we pursue an unskillful option. David and Congleton note that signs we're operating based on patterns and analysis or judgment are when we find ourselves "rerunning" old scripts in our heads ("I'm just not good at math") or filtering current experience through an old, outdated lens ("This new provost is going to be just like the last one"). The pattern we're seeing may indeed be the correct one, but we can't immediately assume that's the case until we see it for what it is: merely a pattern.

Step Two: Label Your Thoughts and Emotions

Unskillful thoughts can crowd our minds so much that there's no room left to examine them. "Just as you call a spade a spade, call a thought a thought and an emotion an emotion. . . . Labeling allows you to see your thoughts and feelings for what they are: transient sources of data that may or may not prove helpful" (David and Congleton 2013, 127). This process is very similar to the sort of labeling that occurs during vipassana meditation.

The idea is to use an objective, non-emotional label to describe something that might otherwise have caused us to become distracted by our emotional response. For example, we might replace the thought "She or he makes me so angry when she or he does that!" with the label *aggravation* or *provocation*. Just because we're being aggravated or provoked, it doesn't mean that we have to respond in any particular way. Once we recognize the stimulus for what it is, we develop greater control over our response. We can make our response more skillful, as illustrated in the following examples:

- "I'm just indulging in that thought again that I'm not doing enough at home or work. I'm being overly critical of myself and need to be as kind and understanding to myself as I try to be to others."
- "I'm making an assumption that my coworker is wrong, and I'm feeling angry again. Anger hasn't been useful in these situations before, and it probably won't be this time either."
- "I keep beating myself up over what I said to Jane. But that was over a year ago, and we've worked things out. I'm reliving ancient history uselessly again. I need to set that aside and move on."

Step Three: Accept Your Thoughts and Emotions as Thoughts and Emotions

After we recognize the stimuli around us for what they are, we can choose to accept them for what they are—or not. As David and Congleton say, just being aware that someone has done something that is making us upset doesn't necessarily solve the problem. "In fact, you may realize just how upset you really are. The important thing is to show yourself (and others) some compassion and examine the reality of the situation. What's going on—both internally and externally?" (David and Congleton 2013, 127–28).

We don't have to act on every thought or emotion we have, but those thoughts and emotions can be cues that a value we care about is being challenged. We don't have to resign ourselves to negativity, but that temptation toward negativity can alert us that there's something unsatisfactory about our current experience that we may wish to address. These types of cues and alerts remind us that we're in a situation that calls for our most skillful approaches to leadership, not mindless reactions that could end up making the problem worse (or even creating a problem where one doesn't currently exist).

Step Four: Act on Your Values

> When you unhook yourself from your difficult thoughts and emotions, you expand your choices. You can decide to act in a way that aligns with your values. . . . Will [your response] help you steer others in a direction that furthers your collective purpose? Are you taking a step toward being the leader you most want to be and living the life you most want to live? (David and Congleton 2013, 128)

In other words, when you prevent yourself from making unskillful decisions through mindlessness, you can decide how and when you want to act. You can make sure that what you decide to do is consistent with those values you listed on the fourth sheet of paper in the exercise you completed earlier. Before you act, you can pause long enough to ask yourself, "Does what I'm about to do align with my leadership principles and priorities?" If it does, then that choice is probably a skillful option. If not, you may want to consider other possible responses.

Peter Post, great grandson of the famous etiquette expert Emily Post, defines respect as "recognizing that how you interact with another person will affect your relationship with that person, and then choosing to take actions that will build relationships rather than injure them" (Post 2012, 4). The type of self-awareness that comes from emotional agility provides us with the insight we need to select the best way to build a solid, respectful relationship with other people, no matter whether the people we're interacting with are students, faculty members, staff members, other administrators, members of the community, or really anyone at all.

AWARENESS OF EXPERIENCE

The second set of non-meditative strategies for developing vipassana that we want to consider, in addition to those aimed at increasing our self-awareness, are those intended to improve our awareness of our experience as it happens. If shamatha seeks to *develop* nonjudgmental awareness of experience as it occurs—the definition of mindfulness that we established in chapter 1—then vipassana seeks to broaden the range of that awareness.

In chapter 2, mindfulness was compared to the type of projector on which zoom and focus were connected: It allows us to expand the range of our awareness without losing clarity. To build on this same metaphor, vipassana is then like switching from that sort of projector to an IMAX or three-dimensional projector. It carries our moment-by-moment awareness to an entirely different level, one that we can easily lose sight of amid the daily pressures of academic leadership.

We can become more aware of our experience by setting an alarm on our phone or computer to alert us periodically (at intervals of perhaps fifteen minutes to an hour) to pause for a moment and notice what's going on around us. What do you hear? You may be surprised to discover that, while you're usually focused on achieving this or that goal in your work, you're surrounded by a rich backdrop of sound. The air-conditioning hums. Birds chirp and scream outside. There are muffled conversations in the hallway. Your computer fan makes a soft whir. Every now and then, a car drives by.

What do you see? You may be in a familiar place like your office, but, if you pay careful attention, you're likely to discover things you've never seen before or perhaps that you once noticed but long ago stopped paying attention to. "Why do we still keep that fax machine over there?" you may wonder. "When was the last time we ever received a fax? Hasn't that file been put away yet? I finished with it more than a week ago."

By paying attention to your environment in this way, you actually accomplish two goals simultaneously: You exercise your ability to remain more aware of your experience, and you notice objects that have been forgotten once they stopped being immediately useful. Since we so often start pursuing the next goal before we have even completed the last, our work spaces can get cluttered by this detritus from previous projects and activities. Vipassana awareness is one means we can pursue in helping ourselves become more organized and efficient.

Of course, the primary purpose of this exercise isn't to get caught up in memories of the past or plans for the future. Rather, it's to become reminded of how little of our environment we typically see and hear when there's so much more available to us. We can use the vipassana technique of labeling to prevent our exercises in awareness from becoming merely inventories of what we need to sort, shred, and put away. (Those exercises can have that benefit as a by-product, but they shouldn't become the entire focus of your practice.)

Another strategy for increasing awareness of our experience non-meditatively is systematic, intentional *unitasking*. For much of our professional lives, we try to multitask. We try to engage in three, four, or even five different processes simultaneously. Multitasking gives us the illusion that we're being efficient, but what we're actually doing is becoming more inefficient at several different activities at once.

Research has repeatedly demonstrated that multitasking is simply not an economical way of getting tasks done. (See, for example, Rosen 2008; Loukopoulos, Dismukes, and Barshi 2009; and Crenshaw 2008.) What we mistake for an ability to devote equal amounts of concentration to several different activities is actually a state known as *continuous partial attention* where we pay a rather superficial amount of attention to the sensory information we're receiving from different tasks.

What typically happens during continuous partial attention is that one of our activities is in the foreground of our minds, several others are in the background, but none of them are really receiving much attention at all. Even worse, we tend to miss things as we rotate among the various activities, bringing each of them in turn to the foreground of our minds. As Robert Cialdini suggests in his book *Pre-Suasion*, "For about a half second during a shift of focus, we experience a mental dead spot, called an *attentional blink*, when we can't register the newly highlighted information consciously" (Cialdini 2016, 29).

Unitasking occurs when we direct our attention, not to several activities simultaneously, but simply and entirely to one at a time. When we write an e-mail, for instance, our full and total attention should be on that e-mail. Chade-Meng Tan recommends that you "[p]ut yourself in the receiver's shoes, pretend you know nothing about the sender's (your) emotional context, pretend that you have a negative bias, and read your e-mail. Revise your e-mail if necessary" (Tan 2012, 226).

What Tan means by "pretend that you have a negative bias" is this: Imagine how someone could *mis*read your e-mail. How could someone who doesn't view the words you're writing in the same way that you intend them misinterpret your remarks, take offense, or become confused?

We typically dash off e-mails without much thought at all. Sometimes the grammar doesn't even make sense. We think that doing so is efficient. But if we consider how much we end up re-doing and re-explaining—not to mention the time required to calm people down who've become upset over a misinterpreted comment—mindful e-mailing is actually a far more economical use of our time.

We can adopt unitasking for other activities as well, such as talking to someone on the phone, reading a report, or checking over a budget. The paradoxical effect of this strategy is that, instead of "shutting out" experiences unrelated to our current activity, we become attuned to how much more there is in our world to experience. We discover nuances in the phone conversation, report, or budget that we never knew existed. That alone can help us become more effective academic leaders.

AWARENESS OF EXPERIENCE AND LEADERSHIP

There are also other ways in which our academic leadership is enhanced by greater awareness of our experience. In a speech before the United Nations General Assembly, Goenka said, "As leaders, we have a responsibility to set an example, to be an inspiration. A sage once said, 'A balanced mind is necessary to balance the unbalanced mind of others'" (Goenka 2000).

You've probably heard the safety instruction from flight attendants, "Put on your own oxygen mask before helping others." Similar advice applies to the area of academic leadership. It's extremely difficult to be of much use to our stakeholders if we're not calm, balanced, and grounded in meaningful priorities ourselves.

Awareness of experience helps us achieve that goal. It makes us more likely to hear others when we listen to them instead of becoming defensive or thinking primarily of how we'll respond. It helps us recognize what members of the faculty, staff, and student body are achieving right now since we're not preoccupied with mistakes from the past and setting the next goal as soon as the current goal's been achieved. It alerts us to when we're becoming annoyed, exhausted, or caught up in the excitement of the moment, thus allowing us to decide if we need to delay our response until after that feeling has passed.

In *The Self-Aware Leader*, Daniel Gallagher and Joseph Costal talk about two important ways in which leaders must be self-aware: they should have *professional self-awareness*, which enables them to recognize their strengths and weaknesses, and *emotional self-awareness*, which helps them to recognize what their "buttons" are before people begin to push them (Gallagher and Costal 2012, 16).

In addition to Gallagher and Costal's recommendations, leaders, particularly academic leaders, should have *social self-awareness*. They should know themselves well enough to understand whether the company of others energizes them (as it tends to do for extroverts) or enervates them (as happens in the case of introverts).

A common assumption used to be that only extroverts could be effective leaders. If you weren't a "people person" and didn't enjoy spending every waking moment in the company of others, then leadership just wasn't your calling.

A great deal of research has demonstrated, however, that introverts can be at least as effective in leadership positions as extroverts; they just lead differently (Cain 2013; Badaracco 2002). If introverts try to imitate the leadership styles of extroverted leaders, they'll end up frustrating themselves and seeming artificial to their stakeholders. If extroverts try to imitate the leadership styles of introverted leaders, they'll feel that they're not accessible enough to those who need them and that their initiatives aren't sufficiently bold.

To be sure, everyone has his or her own leadership style. But in order to embody the style that best suits your personality, you have to be as self-aware as possible. Moreover, to apply that style in the way that's most effective for your stakeholders and institution, you have to be as aware of your experience as possible. A mindful leadership approach that incorporates the vipassana type of awareness can help with both of these aims.

In *The Mindful School Leader* (2015), Valerie Brown and Kirsten Olson recommend an exercise that they call Stepping Stones in Your Leadership Journey. The exercise that Brown and Olson have developed is essentially a self-awareness inventory that helps school leaders reflect on their leadership growth and philosophy.

The approach that they take is just as productive for administrators at a college or university as it would be for those working at the pre-college level. What they recommend is that you start by identifying a few critical moments in your own leadership journey, such as when you first began to envision yourself in leadership roles or when a mentor had a significant impact on your career.

Next, you try to reflect on what those critical moments indicate about you as a person and as an academic leader. Third, you explain these insights to a trusted friend or advisor. Finally, you engage in a conversation with that friend or advisor about what the exercise has made you discover about your leadership style and priorities, the direction you're following in your leadership journey, and recommendations the other person can make about how that journey could be more effective. (For a complete description of this exercise, which contains additional questions for reflection and further guidelines, see Brown and Olson 2015, 185–86.)

One of the important features of the exercise as Brown and Olson have designed it is that you're not merely increasing your self-awareness and the awareness of your environment as an academic leader, you're also required to articulate these thoughts with a partner. Having to explain your observation to another person forces you to clarify your thoughts and to sharpen fuzzy or imprecise ideas. The person you're working with also provides a reality check for you in case your attempt at self-awareness ends up being too self-congratulatory or, at the other extreme of the spectrum, too hard on yourself.

MEETING MINDFULLY WITH VIPASSANA

The two types of awareness we've just explored, self-awareness and awareness of experience, also help academic leaders participate in and conduct meetings more effectively. For example, self-awareness alerts you to the fact that you may be feeling stressed, annoyed, distracted, or agitated as a meeting is about to get under way. You can then use this insight to reground yourself in the matters at hand and to begin to explore the issues before you with curiosity and a sense of greater appreciation for the contributions others are making.

In a similar way, awareness of experience can help you organize a meeting more effectively by clarifying what your intentions are for the group. Is this a regular, procedural meeting, an issue-oriented, problem-solving meeting, or some combination of the two? And if it is the last of these possibilities, are you using people's time in the most effective way possible? Might more get accomplished if routine information were exchanged in some other way (such as by e-mail or on the program's website) so that more time will be available for addressing the issues and problems that are best dealt with in a group setting?

As Dave Kashen, a consultant on how to make meetings more effective, describes the challenge we face as leaders,

> Most meetings have a number of parts to them, but typically those parts are not distinguished so the meeting feels like a big blur. People experience the meeting as one continuous conversation until it abruptly ends so they can rush off to their next meeting. Imagine a mechanic who looks under the hood of a car and just sees one big blob of engine. He wouldn't be very effective at making it run smoothly or fixing what's broken. Different parts of the engine require different tools. (Kashen 2014)

Mindful leaders help those in attendance at meetings "distinguish the parts" of the meeting, to use Kashen's words, and thus apply the right mental "tool" to the right problem at hand.

Awareness of experience thus also means being aware of the needs and motivations of the other people at the meeting. If your group includes several people who are reluctant to speak in front of others (particularly those with very strong opinions), you may need to be more proactive in drawing them out and soliciting their views. If certain members seem disengaged from the topic under discussion, it may be useful to discover where their interests lie and to seek (where possible) closer connections between those interests and the topic.

It can also be productive to check in with different members of the committee when they arrive, helping them make a smooth transition from whatever it was they were doing earlier to the subject matter that will now be discussed at the meeting. So often, people rush from teaching to research to more teaching to a meeting that they can feel fragmented and thus do not make productive contributions to the meeting. By assisting committee members with this transition, you'll enable people to focus better on the issues that need to be addressed, thus increasing their awareness and general mindfulness as well.

As the meeting progresses, pay attention to the body language of everyone in the room. Can you tell if anyone is upset, disengaged, or angry? Are the members in attendance truly listening to one another or merely making set speeches without paying attention to their colleagues? As an academic leader, you can assist others with their own awareness by gently summarizing key points from time to time, seeking points of consensus that others may not see, and keeping the meeting moving forward by asking key questions at appropriate intervals.

FINAL REMARKS ON VIPASSANA

Before we conclude this brief discussion of vipassana, it may be useful to add one proviso. If you find that you're so interested in this approach to meditation that you decide to attend one of the ten-day retreats offered at a vipassana meditation center that operates in the Goenka tradition, do your homework carefully.

Although the vast majority of those who participate in these programs find them beneficial (at times even life changing), they're definitely not for everyone. Some attendees, particularly those with Western backgrounds, find Goenka's approach too inflexible. They come away from the experience feeling that there was an attempt to indoctrinate them in a negative worldview and a specific religious philosophy. Descriptions such as "cult-like" and "boot camp" are sometimes used. (See, for example, Spiritual Matters 2013; phen375cost29 n.d.; and Singh 2007.) Others find the obligation to remain almost totally silent for the entire duration of the retreat an impossible burden to bear.

In any case, the video and audio lectures in which Goenka explains his approach are available for purchase (Goenka 2006, 2008). Studying these lectures and practicing both the shamatha and vipassana techniques for periods far longer than the five-minute blocks recommended in this book might be regarded as useful preparations for the challenges of immersing yourself in a full ten-day retreat.

KEY POINTS FROM CHAPTER 3

- Vipassana or insight meditation is a technique that directs one's attention toward current experience such as the sensations that are occurring in all parts of one's body.
- Many of the benefits of vipassana meditation can be achieved through exercises that increase a person's self-awareness or the awareness of his or her experience.
- Self-awareness provides greater insights into our emotional states, mere passing thoughts, and values so that it becomes easier to avoid being distracted by irrelevant issues and to be guided by those principles that are truly important to us.

- Respect, when seen from a mindfulness perspective, shouldn't be confused with deference or submissiveness. It is instead a constant awareness that what we say and do affects our relationships with others and a commitment to building rather than weakening relationships.
- Awareness of experience strengthens our ability to recognize what is going on around us without immediately reacting to or judging it.
- Awareness of experience also helps us break unproductive habits like multitasking and replace them with more skillful habits like unitasking.
- Vipassana practices, regardless of whether they are meditative or non-meditative in nature, enable us to be more aware of our own needs as academic leaders and also the needs, emotional states, and perspectives of our stakeholders.
- Vipassana practices also enable us to accomplish more in meetings because they help us remain aware of our own feelings, thoughts, and values as well as the feelings, thoughts, and values of others in the room.

EXERCISES TO COMPLETE BEFORE PROCEEDING TO CHAPTER 4

1. If you find yourself getting bored by the vipassana meditation technique described in this chapter, you can vary it a bit by trying one or more of the following alterations:
    - Pay attention to only one sensation per scan: sounds, bodily sensations, light, and so on.
    - Give full attention to only one body part per session.
    - Slowly move your hand and note the sensations that result. Try this exercise first with your eyes closed then with your eyes open.
    - Let your hands settle in your lap. Alternate your focus between the sensations of your hands and the sensations of your seat in the chair.
    - Engage in a variation of the walking meditation we encountered at the end of chapter 2: This time as you walk, note each different sensation in turn. Label each sight, sound, feeling, taste, and smell. Do so slowly and systematically rather than trying to be thorough. If you happen to miss a sensation because you're noting another one right then, that's okay.
    - Practice a variation of the massage meditation we encountered at the end of chapter 2: Notice wherever the masseuse's fingers and hands come into contact with your body, but also label the other sounds and impressions you notice. Don't judge each experience; simply become aware of it, and then proceed to the next sensation.
    - Practice *mindful eating*: Sometime when you're eating alone, rather than letting your mind wander or listening to music, let your mind

rest on each small bite of food you take. Savor it completely so that you experience every aspect of it, most particularly its aroma, taste, warmth, and texture. You can do a miniature version of mindful eating by simply taking a single piece of fruit or candy, studying it closely to experience everything about it before you put it in your mouth, and then slowly, mindfully savoring it. In Mindfulness-Based Stress Reduction, this practice is often done with a raisin, but almost any food will do. (For a full discussion of mindful eating and the raisin meditation, see Williams, Penman, and Kabat-Zinn 2011, 55, 972–79; and Salzburg and Goldstein 2001, 116–21.)

2. Similarly, if you want to try some variations of the non-meditative approaches to vipassana that were explained in this chapter, consider the following activities:

- Study the same object consistently over several days. For this exercise, it's probably best to select an object of reasonable complexity: something with varied colors and textures and that's composed of several parts is best. Each day for two weeks, study that object intensely for five minutes at a time. Try to observe something each day that you hadn't noticed before.
- Practice *mindful listening*. Each day, choose a song you've never heard before and then listen to it several times in succession. Simply pay attention to it; don't judge it, deciding whether you like it or don't like it. Instead, experience its structure, texture, and feeling.
- Practice *mindful engagement*. Have a conversation with someone you're familiar with but whom you don't know particularly well, trying to find out as much as you can about the other person without seeming to pry into overly personal areas. See if you can determine how that person views the world. What's most important in life to this person? How is the person like you and unlike you? As in all of these exercises, merely try to observe and learn. Don't judge.

REFERENCES

Badaracco, J. 2002. *Leading Quietly: An Unorthodox Guide to Doing the Right Thing*. Boston: Harvard Business School Press.

Brockman, J. (Ed.) 2006. *What We Believe but Cannot Prove: Today's Leading Thinkers on Science in the Age of Certainty*. New York: Harper Perennial.

Brown, V., and K. Olson. 2015. *The Mindful School Leader: Practices to Transform Your Leadership and School*. Thousand Oaks, CA: Corwin.

Cain, S. 2013. *Quiet: The Power of Introverts in a World That Can't Stop Talking.* New York: Broadway Paperbacks.

Cialdini, R. 2016. *Pre-Suasion: A Revolutionary Way to Influence and Persuade.* New York: Simon & Schuster.

Crenshaw, D. 2008. *The Myth of Multitasking: How Doing It All Gets Nothing Done.* San Francisco, CA: Jossey-Bass.

David, S., and C. Congleton. 2013, November. "Emotional Agility: Effective Leaders Are Mindful of Their Inner Experiences—but Not Ruled by Them." *Harvard Business Review* 91, no. 11 (November): 125–28.

Gallagher, D., and J. Costal. 2012. *The Self-Aware Leader.* Alexandria, VA: ASTD Press.

Glickman, M. 2002. *Beyond the Breath: Extraordinary Mindfulness through Whole-Body Vipassana Meditation.* North Clarendon, VT: Journey.

Goenka, S. N. 2000. "Address to the UN Assembly: Universal Spirituality for Peace." Japan Vipassana Association, August 29, 2000. Retrieved from https://www.jp.dhamma.org/deep-archive/vipassana-in-the-society/un-speech/.

Goenka, S. N. 2006. *Dhamma Discourses* [DVDs]. Maharashtra, India: Vipassana Research Institute.

Goenka, S. N. 2008. *Dhamma Discourses: From the Ten-Day Vipassana Course* [CDs]. Onalaska, WA: Pariyatti Audio Editions.

Hart, W. 1987. *The Art of Living: Vipassana Meditation as Taught by S. N. Goenka.* New York: HarperOne.

Kashen, D. 2014. "5 Simple Steps toward More Mindful Meetings." *Fast Company*, August 4, 2015. Retrieved from https://www.fastcompany.com/3033897/5-simple-steps-towards-more-mindful-meetings.

Loukopoulos, L. D., K. Dismukes, and I. Barshi. 2009. *The Multi-Tasking Myth: Handling Complexity in Real-World Operations.* Farnham, UK: Ashgate.

phen375cost29. n.d. "Criticisms of Goenka's Vipassana Meditation Centres [document upload]." Scribd. Retrieved from https://www.scribd.com/document/264531236/Criticisms-of-Goenka-s-Vipassana-Meditation-Centres.

Post, P. 2012. *Essential Manners for Men*, 2nd ed. New York, NY: HarperCollins.

Rosen, C. 2008. "The Myth of Multitasking." *The New Atlantis* 20 (April): 105–10. Retrieved from https://www.thenewatlantis.com/publications/the-myth-of-multitasking.

Salzburg, S., and J. Goldstein. 2001. *Insight Meditation Workbook.* Boulder, CO: Sounds True.

Singh, H. 2007. "A Critique of Vipassana Meditation as Taught by Mr S N Goenka," July 20, 2007. http://eldar.cz/kangaroo/mirror/vipassana-critique.pdf.

Spiritual Matters. 2013. "The 10 day (Goenka) Vipassana Retreat: A Warning," August 15, 2013. https://morespiritualmatters.wordpress.com/2013/08/15/the-10-day-vipassana-retreat-a-warning/.

Tan, C.-M. 2012. *Search Inside Yourself: Increase Productivity, Creativity and Happiness.* New York: HarperCollins.

University of Pennsylvania: Authentic Happiness Questionnaire Center. 2017. Retrieved from https://www.authentichappiness.sas.upenn.edu/testcenter.

Williams, J. M. G., D. Penman, and J. Kabat-Zinn. 2011. *Mindfulness: An Eight-Week Plan for Finding Peace in a Frantic World*. Emmaus, PA: Rodale.

RESOURCES

Goenka, S. N. 2003. *Meditation Now: Inner Peace through Inner Wisdom*. Seattle, WA: Vipassana Research.

Goenka, S. N., and W. Hart. 2000. *The Discourse Summaries: Talks from a Ten-Day Course in Vipassana Meditation*. Seattle, WA: Vipassana Research Publications.

Chapter 4

Mantra

Expanding Creativity

The term *mantra* is quite common in English, although few people are aware of its etymology. For instance, we hear expressions like "'If you're going to fly, fly first class.' That was Alice's mantra," or, "Our college's mantra was 'The students always come first.'" But what does the word *mantra* actually mean? Are the examples we just cited true mantras? And if they are, how do they fit into a program of mindful academic leadership?

The first thing we need to realize is that the word *mantra*, like the word *shamatha*, is derived from Sanskrit, that classical Indian language that originated sometime during the second millennium BCE. Its roots are *manas* meaning "mind" (cognate with the Latin word *mens/mentis* and thus related to the English word *mental*) and the noun suffix *–tra* designating an instrument or tool.

A mantra is thus linguistically a "mind tool," and that's a useful way to think of it. We can use a mantra as a mental device to remind us of whatever it is we want to keep in our awareness such as the experience of the present moment—the goals we had in the shamatha and vipassana approaches—or other important concepts like generosity, professionalism, and creativity.

In Eastern philosophy, the type of "mind tool" described by the term *mantra* is a specific word, syllable, or sound that induces a desired state or results in a desired action. In the West, many people were first introduced to the idea of mantras through the work of the *Maharishi Mahesh Yogi* (1918–2008), whose students included many celebrities such as the musicians George Harrison (as well as, to a lesser extent, the other members of the Beatles) and Ravi Shankar.

The maharishi called the use of mantras for mindfulness and enlightenment *transcendental meditation*, a registered trademark for an approach still used in centers all over the world (Maharishi Foundation 2017). There's even a university in Fairfield, Iowa, the Maharishi University of Management, that has applied the techniques of transcendental meditation across the curriculum.

In transcendental meditation, students are assigned an individualized mantra that consists of a sound having no immediately obvious meaning to them. They then practice meditating on this sound with their eyes closed twice a day for sessions of about fifteen to twenty minutes each. Although the mantras that are assigned are indeed personalized, there are patterns to them, and those patterns have changed several times since the maharishi first introduced the program of transcendental meditation. At certain times, the sounds assigned were based on the meditator's age; at other times, the selection was done on the basis of age and gender.

The popularity and (for many) the effectiveness of transcendental meditation led several scholars to develop an equivalent form of mantra meditation that was free from the Western philosophical terminology and religious context that still imbued the version of this mindfulness technique as taught by the Maharishi Mahesh Yogi.

In 1975, Herbert Benson, a Harvard cardiologist who founded the Mind/Body Medical Institute at Massachusetts General Hospital in Boston, experimented with transcendental meditation and tried to develop a simplified and secular alternative. Although the name he gave his technique was the respiratory one method or ROM, it became popularly known as the relaxation response, after the title of the book he wrote describing it (Benson 1975). Benson saw the relaxation response as a way to reverse what the physiologist Walter Cannon had dubbed the *fight-or-flight response*, the state in which a person's body autonomously prepares to confront or avoid a stressful situation.

With the relaxation one method or relaxation response, the practitioner adopts a comfortable position, relaxes the muscles throughout the body, and then mentally repeats the word "one" every time he or she exhales. As distracting thoughts arise, the practitioner is encouraged simply to ignore them and return to meditating on the word "one." Other mantras may be adopted if a person finds some other syllable to be more relaxing. Benson firmly believed that it wasn't the content of the mantra that mattered, merely the routine, repetitive reflection on a single sound.

Patricia Carrington, a psychologist at Princeton University and the Robert Wood Johnson Medical School at Rutgers University, developed an approach rather similar to that of Benson, experimenting with a list of one hundred Sanskrit, Hebrew, and English words that she eventually reduced to sixteen that her students rated as particularly soothing. Among the mantras Carrington used in her approach were *ah-nam* (which she based on the Sanskrit term *anāman*, meaning *nameless*), *shi-rim* (Hebrew for *songs*, as in *shir ha shirim*, "song of songs"), and *ram-ah* (based on the name of Hindu deity Rama).

So, while neither Benson nor Carrington used mantras that were technically meaningless, their sounds either were unfamiliar to the practitioner (Carrington 1998, 83–84, 154–57) or they became *so* familiar by constant repetition that their literal meaning was almost irrelevant (Benson 1975).

Carrington's approach, which she called clinically standardized meditation, involved selecting one of her recommended mantras (or one of the student's own creations), allowing the eyes to rest on a pleasant object such as a plant or a comforting color on the wall, and then repeating the mantra. Carrington had her students begin by repeating their mantras out loud, gradually saying them more and more softly until they became a whisper and, finally, a subvocalization in their own thoughts.

Students were encouraged to approach their mantras playfully and to allow them to progress however they liked. For instance, the "sound" of the mantras within their thoughts might spontaneously grow "louder" at some moments and "softer" at others. Students could also stretch the mantras out during some repetitions or speed them up and contract them during others.

Like transcendental meditation, both the relaxation response and clinically standardized meditation are practiced in sessions of about fifteen to twenty minutes, twice a day. But they each also have their own unique (some might even say peculiar) features. Benson encouraged meditators not to practice ROM within two hours of a meal because he believed that digestion might interfere with the relaxation process. Carrington urged people to include a two- to three-minute "cool down" period after each meditation session, where they would remain seated and relaxed but not actively meditating.

THE CHOICE OF A MANTRA

While both Benson and Carrington recommended specific mantras, they did allow students to create their own. So, if you are interested in practicing some form of mantra meditation, how do you go about selecting which mantra to use? The first thing you have to determine is whether you find it more effective to adopt a meaningless mantra (which causes your single point awareness to rest upon a *sound*) or a meaningful mantra (which causes your single point awareness to rest upon an *idea*). Both approaches have their advantages.

Meaningless mantras serve as complements of and extensions to the shamatha and vipassana techniques that we explored earlier: They ground your awareness in the present moment and train you to be more aware of and less instantly judgmental about what you experience as it occurs. Some people prefer the use of meaningless mantras to meditation on the breath or physical sensations because they find that their minds wander less with this approach. Others have the opposite experience. Because the sound or syllable they use for meditation has no meaning, they quickly find it boring, and so their minds wander more.

You simply have to try the technique to see whether you find it useful. Keep in mind, however, the proviso we've mentioned before: Just because your mind wanders, that's not a sign that you're not using the technique properly; remembering to guide your mind back to the breath, sensation, or mantra *is* the technique.

Meaningful mantras, on the other hand, can cause you to elevate an idea so that it becomes foremost in your consciousness. It functions a little bit like hypnosis (to choose a positive example) or brainwashing (to choose a negative one) by "reprogramming" your thoughts so that some important concept guides you, not only when you're consciously aware of it, but even when you're not actively thinking about it.

Advocates of the counseling approach known as *cognitive behavioral therapy* sometimes speak of *making the covert overt*. In other words, by working with a professional counselor, patients are guided to understanding how negative thoughts and perspectives that they may not even be aware of affect their feelings and actions. Meaningful mantras work in almost the opposite fashion. They *make the overt covert* by causing your reflex, autopilot responses to be influenced by a specific idea or concept.

To use the language introduced in chapter 1, meaningful mantras provide you with a new heuristic your mind can use to make judgments automatically when you feel it's appropriate to do so. One way of thinking about the difference, then, is that meaningless mantras help improve our mindfulness, while meaningful mantras help improve our autopilot. As we'll see, that's a bit of a simplification, but it provides a useful initial framework as we explore mantra meditation in greater detail.

We'll experiment with both meaningless and meaningful mantras so that you can decide which option you prefer. And we'll start with meaningless mantras. The key to choosing an effective mantra of this type is to select a sound or series of sounds that is utterly devoid of intellectual or emotional content for you. That doesn't mean, of course, that the sound may not have meaning for *someone*. It's virtually impossible to select a sound that doesn't mean something in some language somewhere.

But for you, the mantra should be a sound that doesn't remind you of anything or make you feel any particular way. To go a step further, for the purposes of mindful academic leadership, a good mantra shouldn't even be particularly soothing. After all, our goal is greater awareness and more effective leadership, not relaxation for its own sake.

But how do you find a mantra that contains absolutely no meaning or emotional content for you? One way is simply to invent one. Experiment with different sounds until you come up with a one- or two-syllable sound that doesn't remind you of any word in any language that you know and that doesn't make you feel any particular way when you say it or subvocalize it in your head. A second way is to choose a mantra from the various lists of nonsense syllables that were developed for purposes other than meditation. Perhaps the most famous of these lists is associated with the work of the German psychologist Hermann Ebbinghaus (1850–1909).

Ebbinghaus wanted to discover how memory functioned, and so he developed lists of nonsense syllables that he memorized in a random order and then tried to determine how long he could remember them. Ebbinghaus's most famous experiments involved *trigrams* (groups of three letters) that consisted either of three consonants (CCC) or two consonants separated by a vowel (CVC).

In many ways, Ebbinghaus's CVC pattern provides the perfect formula for a meaningless mantra: It creates a short syllable that's easy to pronounce or subvocalize, and the possible combinations are so numerous that practitioners have no trouble finding a syllable that is completely devoid of meaning to them.

Table 4.1, for example, contains a list of some suggested CVC combinations, including many of those that Ebbinghaus used in his experiments.

We can also expand our choices by including syllables that, in English pronunciation, contain a consonant digraph (two consonants that are used to represent a single sound such as *sh*, *ch*, or *ng*), diphthong (a vowel sound that glides into another vowel or semivowel such as *aw* or *oy*), or consonant blend (two consonants pronounced in rapid succession such as *bl*, *cr*, or *st*). With these added possibilities, we can create syllables such as those in table 4.2.

Table 4.1 Suggested CVC Combinations

bec	sen	mub	tum
dod	mip	sar	vep
guf	gos	nac	yot
hej	lut	tuj	zux
jik	pav	vak	baz
kol	hiz	zel	wub
lum	tob	bim	ral
mep	ruc	yon	faj
nis	vad	wup	vif
tuv	sef	bas	ror
wib	kig	gox	jad
yoc	yoj	huz	suf
zud	zuk	seb	nej
baf	bal	mim	nen
deg	hin	lod	pob
fij	gat	kuf	ret
gok	kev	rik	lig

Table 4.2 Additional Syllables

shub	zash	hosh	flayb
chon	shawm	tresh	yarm
hesh	blor	pleng	doys
guch	plawm	hoyd	sherm
shuf	twef	stawd	crom

Before beginning the exercise as follows, select the mantra that you'll use, either by consulting lists of mantras used in approaches such as transcendental meditation or clinically standardized meditation that you can find online or by inventing your own.

MANTRA MEDITATION #1: MEANINGLESS MANTRAS

For the first method of mantra meditation that we'll use, these are the steps that you'll follow:

1. Complete the standard meditation preparation as described in chapter 2.
2. Pause for a moment to set aside your normal work and activities, focusing your attention on the fact that you're about to meditate. If it helps to do so, practice the shamatha technique for several breaths until you feel calm and prepared to begin the exercise.
3. Set a timer for five minutes.
4. Mentally recite the mantra.
5. Pause slightly.
6. Then mentally recite it again, finding your own rhythm between each time you subvocalize your mantra.
7. If you like, you can combine your mantra with your breathing. For instance, you might mentally recite your mantra as you inhale and let your thoughts go where they may as you exhale. But you can also use your mantra independently of your breathing if you find that easier. No matter which approach you adopt, however, don't force or control your breath. Simply breathe naturally.
8. Whenever you realize that your attention has wandered off and that you've been thinking of things other than your mantra, simply guide your attention gently back to the technique.
9. Continue this process until the timer goes off.

Reviewing the Experience

The goal of meditating with a meaningless mantra isn't, of course, to become more mindful of the mantra. It's to become more mindful of whatever you experience as it occurs. In this way, mantra meditation complements and extends the other types of single point meditation that we've considered. If you find meditation useful as a way of grounding yourself in experience as it occurs, you can thus begin to develop a customized technique that best suits your individual needs.

As your ability to maintain longer and longer periods of mindfulness increases—and as you make more room in your day for meditation because you find it valuable—you might consider an individualized plan that consists of five minutes of shamatha meditation, followed by a longer period of vipassana or mantra meditation. One of the advantages of exploring several different techniques is that it enables you to continue the methods that work for you, discard the others, and discover an approach that suits your temperament and workday.

MANTRA MEDITATION #2: MEANINGFUL MANTRAS

As we move from meaningless to meaningful mantras, we're also beginning to encounter a different type of meditation, one that causes us to become more mindful, not merely of the present moment, but of some idea, feeling, or goal that's important to us. A great deal of meditation within religious traditions involves meaningful mantras. The practitioner meditates on the passions of Christ, the compassion of the Buddha, or the oneness of the universe.

The goal, therefore, is to increase the practitioner's awareness on the object of meditation even when not actively meditating. If single point meditation seeks to redirect our attention to experience as it occurs, meaningful mantras seek to redirect our attention to something important that we feel we may be overlooking in our daily lives.

Like all approaches to meditation, there is no reason why meaningful mantras *must* be tied to a religious tradition. They're useful for any idea about which we wish to remain more mindful after our meditation practice is over. Serenity, visionary leadership, creativity, perseverance in the face of adversity, and other such concepts can all be the goal of meditating on a meaningful mantra. We'll begin to consider how this idea might work by applying meaningful mantras to an area that many academic leaders say they struggle with: coping with the pressures of their positions.

The mantras that we'll explore for this exercise fall into two groups: one-syllable mantras that you can recite mentally as you inhale (letting your thoughts go wherever they may as you exhale) and two-syllable mantras that provide you with one syllable to subvocalize as you inhale and another as you exhale.

If you've been experimenting with the techniques introduced so far, you've probably developed a preference for either a meditation "anchor" for your awareness full time throughout a session or one that alternates periods of single point awareness with free-flowing thought. Use that preference to select which type of meaningful mantra you'll use during the next exercise.

Here are the one-syllable mantras you may choose from:

- hush
- peace
- life
- love
- calm
- am
- sea
- care
- less
- sigh
- soft
- joy

The two-syllable mantras for this exercise are as follows:

- serene
- release
- compose
- relax
- persist
- placid
- relieve
- sedate
- unwind
- let go
- simple
- tranquil

After you select the mantra you'll use for this exercise, follow these steps:

1. Complete the standard meditation preparation as described in chapter 2.
2. Pause for a moment to set aside your normal work and activities, focusing your attention on the fact that you're about to meditate. If it helps to do so, practice the shamatha technique for several breaths until you feel calm and prepared to begin the exercise.

3. Set a timer for five minutes.
4. Mentally recite the mantra. If you selected a one-syllable mantra, subvocalize it as you breathe in, letting your thoughts go wherever they like as you breathe out. If you selected a two-syllable mantra, mentally recite the first syllable as you inhale, the second syllable as you exhale.
5. In either case, don't force or control your breath. Simply breathe naturally.
6. Whenever you realize that your attention has wandered off and that you've been thinking of things other than your mantra, simply guide your attention gently back to the technique.
7. Continue this process until the timer goes off.

Most people find that, after completing this exercise, they're temporarily calmer than they were before. Initially, that feeling of relaxation doesn't last very long. In fact, it's likely to dissipate the moment that the person returns to the stress of the job. But for those who find this technique useful, the ability to retain that sense of calm grows with practice. As practitioners engage in this technique for longer and longer sessions, they tend to find that at least some level of calm remains with them throughout the entire day.

Keep in mind, however, that this result is not instant. You're only likely to realize that level of continued relaxation if you build to sessions of fifteen to twenty minutes a day and practice the technique daily for a month or more.

NON-MEDITATIVE USES OF MANTRAS

Does it mean, therefore, that mantras are useless if you find that you don't have that kind of time to devote to a meditation practice or aren't interested in meditation at all? Certainly not. Just as with the other techniques we've discussed, there are non-meditative alternatives to mantra meditation that can convey most, if not all, of this method's benefits.

As we saw at the beginning of this chapter, people commonly use the term *mantra* to refer to a repeated saying or guiding principle in someone's life. This type of mantra can provide a welcome degree of focus and consistency when so much of modern life seems to be trying to pull us in a thousand directions at once.

One non-meditative use of mantras is thus to select some term or statement that you believe grounds you in what's important and maintains your focus in the midst of distractions. The mantra could be a single word such as *courage, determination, excellence, integrity, transparency, accessibility,* or *service* (an extensive list of potential leadership mantras appears in table 4.3), or it could be a statement or quotation that you find particularly meaningful.

Table 4.3 Possible Single-Word Leadership Mantras

action	enthusiasm	love	self-control
altruism	equality	loyalty	self-esteem
appreciation	ethics	manners	selflessness
aspiration	excellence	mastery	sensibility
assertiveness	fairness	mercy	serenity
caring	faith	merit	sincerity
character	flexibility	moderation	skill
charisma	focus	modesty	sportsmanship
charm	forgiveness	mood	steadfastness
cheer	friendship	morals	success
citizenship	generosity	motivation	sympathy
civility	gentleness	neatness	tact
commitment	goodness	obedience	talent
common sense	grace	observantness	teamwork
community	gratitude	open-mindedness	tenacity
compassion	guidance	optimism	tenderness
confidence	happiness	patience	thoughtfulness
consideration	harmony	patriotism	thriftiness
cooperation	honesty	peace	tolerance
courage	honor	perseverance	tranquility
courtesy	hope	persistence	trustworthiness
creativity	humility	philanthropy	truth
curiosity	humor	principle	understanding
decency	idealism	priorities	unity
dependability	imagination	promptness	values
determination	impartiality	punctuality	veracity
devotion	ingenuity	quality	versatility
dignity	innovation	quick	vigilance
diligence	insight	refinement	virtue
diplomacy	inspiration	resilience	vision
discipline	integrity	resolution	warmth
discretion	judgment	resourcefulness	willingness
dynamism	justice	respect	wisdom
empathy	kindness	responsibility	work
encouragement	laughter	restraint	yearning
endurance	leadership	reverence	zeal
energy	legitimacy	righteousness	zest

You then maintain your awareness of this word or saying by reflecting on it frequently or surrounding yourself with it by including it in

- the signature box you use in e-mails,
- a sticky note on the side of your computer screen,
- a plaque placed on your desk or hung on the wall of your office, or
- alerts that you set to appear periodically on your cell phone.

Eventually, this personal mantra simply becomes part of your standard operating procedure. It will occur to you naturally every time you start feeling tense, have an important decision to make, or are having a bad day.

Successories, a company that produces office decorations, has even made a thriving business out of creating posters, awards, and art objects that incorporate personal mantras in this way. Many of the products developed by Successories consist of a motivational term like *teamwork* or *leadership*, a brief statement summarizing a key aspect of that term, and a photograph somehow related to that concept.

Even though motivational posters are frequently ridiculed as superficial and manipulative—there is even a competing firm called Despair, Inc. that satirizes the Successories style with sarcastic, "demotivational" posters—their basic concept has validity: By directing our attention to a key concept repeatedly, we're more likely to incorporate that concept into our choices and actions. It's one thing, however, to use a motto or mantra in this way for your own personal motivation, but it's something else entirely when a supervisor uses this tactic in an effort to manipulate employees into working harder.

Another non-meditative approach to mantras that is often ridiculed even though it's effective is the use of *affirmations*. Affirmations are positive statements we make to ourselves as a way of providing encouragement and increasing self-esteem. A popular example of an affirmation occurs in the 2011 film *The Help* when the maid Aibileen Clark repeatedly tells her employer's often neglected daughter, "You is smart. You is kind. You is important" (Al-Mazrouei and Taylor 2011). Aibileen encourages the girl to repeat and internalize these sentiments, and it becomes clear later in the movie that she's done so.

The cartoonist Scott Adams, whose daily strip *Dilbert* often casts a cynical eye on the latest trends in leadership and the self-esteem movement, applies none of this cynicism to the power of affirmation, which he believes has helped him significantly in his life and career. He believes that affirmations can be a powerful device for focusing one's awareness and may even serve as a form of self-hypnosis, causing the person who uses them regularly to reprogram or "rewire" his or her thought processes (Adams 2013, 154–57, 225–29). He credits affirmations with helping him recover his voice after a serious health condition and eventually bringing him the level of career success that he hoped for.

Like motivational posters, however, affirmations are easy to satirize. The comedian (and eventually senator from the state of Minnesota) Al Franken did exactly that through his character Stuart Smalley, a self-help guru whose most famous affirmation is "I'm good enough, I'm smart enough, and doggone it, people like me!" (Franken and Beattie 1992).

Like any technique used for personal development, some people will find the use of affirmations helpful; others won't. But if you do decide to give this technique a try, realize that what you're using is essentially a non-meditative mantra. You're adopting a word or phrase that you repeat to yourself regularly as a means of directing your awareness toward some insight that may otherwise get lost as you deal with the day-to-day challenges of life.

Some suitable affirmations and mantras for academic leaders include the following:

- I treat everyone I meet with respect and understanding.
- I am as transparent as possible about as much as possible as often as possible.
- Each challenge I face is not a crisis. It's an opportunity for me to demonstrate leadership.
- A leader's greatest duty is to empower others.
- I will see the potential in each person I meet.

The precise affirmation you use will depend on what important thoughts or feelings you lose sight of most. If you're feeling overwhelmed, select an affirmation that reminds you to remain calm and in control. If you tend to respond to others with anger, choose one that reminds you to be compassionate, and so on. Envision the version of yourself that you'd like others to see, and create a mantra that reminds you to live into those possibilities.

GEARING UP RATHER THAN CALMING DOWN

Occasionally, someone will say in a workshop on mindful academic leadership, "All of this seems well and good if you're interested in stress reduction or managing your anger in an academic setting, but that's not my problem. I actually feel that I may be too passive and low-energy as an academic leader. My goal is to become more assertive, or to 'gear up' rather than to 'calm down.' Does mindful academic leadership do anything to address that need?"

Certainly it can be argued that both the meditative and non-meditative approaches to shamatha and vipassana focus more on becoming less immediately reactive to stimuli and thus focus more on relieving stress, anger, and hostility than on promoting stronger or more aggressive responses. But if you are worried that your leadership style is too hands-off and are seeking a more energized approach to dealing with challenges, then mantra techniques may be a more suitable avenue toward mindful academic leadership.

Since meaningful mantras can consist of whatever content you need most, the modification you need to make to this method is merely selecting a mantra that guides your awareness toward greater activity and intervention rather than toward greater calm and increased observation. Here are a few suitable mantras for this purpose:

- "Just do it" (the trademarked Nike slogan).
- Say *yes* to opportunity. Say *no* to resistance.
- If you can't get out of it, get into it.
- "Own the moment. Own your space" (attributed to Andrena Sawyer, the president of P.E.R.K. Consulting).
- Raise your expectations, not your voice.
- Nothing is impossible.
- "Be a good person, but don't waste your time trying to prove it" (Coelho 2017).

Or, you might consider using one or more of the following affirmations:

- I will become more assertive.
- I feel powerful and confident.
- I am in charge of my choices.
- I believe in and trust myself.
- I see criticism as information that empowers me.
- I express my feelings and opinions honestly and openly.
- I have a powerful positive mental attitude.
- I am optimistic and in control.
- I am the designer of my destiny.
- I know my own value and abilities.
- I will stand up for what I believe in.

As with any meaningful mantra or personal affirmation, the goal is to remind yourself what you will need to remember in order to achieve the goals you have. What is appropriate for you may not be appropriate for a colleague, even if he or she is also working on how to become more assertive and less passive. You are more likely to find the right formula by asking yourself, "What is it that I feel I'm lacking? How can I remind myself that I actually do have that since I have more resources at my disposal than I sometimes believe?"

USING MANTRAS TO IMPROVE ACADEMIC LEADERSHIP

By maintaining our awareness of what we believe we need in order to succeed as academic leaders, mantras help us to distinguish the truly important from the "noise" that surrounds us in our jobs. But some observers have taken this connection between mantras and effective leadership to an entirely different level.

For instance, Dana A. Oliver in his book *Mantra Leadership: Don't Become the Emperor with No Clothes* believes that an important practice of effective leaders is "consistency in messaging" (Oliver 2014, 14). We have a tendency to make leadership seem more complex and mysterious than it actually is. And so, many leaders careen from one management fad to the next: Total Quality Management gets replaced by Process Reengineering, which, in turn, gets replaced by Six Sigma. The result is that the leaders themselves lose focus, and their vision for the companies or organizations they lead gets diluted.

Oliver's alternative view is that the essence of good leadership can be reduced to fourteen key principles, including "Spend fifteen percent of your time on innovation," "Say good morning," and "If everything is important, nothing is" (Oliver 2014, 33–36, 71–74, and 87–102). Even if you disagree with some of the principles Oliver outlines, his basic approach has merit. A great part of what mindful academic leaders are trying to do is maintain their focus on what's important without being distracted by trends that suddenly emerge in the literature of higher education leadership without having sound, practical utility in what they actually do as administrators.

Leadership mantras are touchstones we can use to clarify for ourselves whether an idea has merit and for others what it is we truly believe in. As your own mindful leadership mantra, you might consider adopting one or more of the following:

- Just because you can doesn't mean you should.
- Hope is not a strategy.
- "To handle yourself, use your head; to handle others, use your heart" (attributed to Eleanor Roosevelt).
- The leader's goal is to produce more leaders, not more followers.
- If you don't have enough time to listen to people, you don't have time to lead.

As with the other mantras that we've considered, a good leadership touchstone should be something that's genuinely important to you but that also is not already so integrated in your behavior that you never need to remind yourself of it. It can be a difficult balance to achieve, but the goal is to find a concept that accurately reflects your core principles yet still remains a bit aspirational.

USING MANTRAS TO INCREASE CREATIVITY

The adoption of a leadership mantra, motto, or slogan is not an attempt to make our decision-making more automatic. To the contrary, mindful academic leadership seeks to make us intentional about the choices we make, using heuristics and autopilot when that's helpful, but not all the time. And if we're careful in adopting the right mantras to guide us, they can even help us increase the creativity and innovation we bring to our positions.

For example, until it became trite through constant repetition, the injunction to "think outside the box" served as a useful reminder to leaders that logical, sequential thinking and relying on the lessons of the past may get in the way of solving a new and unexpected problem. Many a discussion that was going nowhere because people assumed, "We can't do *that*," has been given way to new insights because someone's mantra was, "But what if we could?"

Leadership mantras are particularly useful in fostering creative approaches because they don't recommend a specific solution; they instead remind us to consider alternative approaches before choosing a specific course of action. As such, they encourage mindfulness because they help us avoid the trap of taking a course of action merely because it's familiar or obvious. But even more than this, they encourage us to stretch ourselves, to accept the possibility that there are better solutions waiting for us if we decide to pursue them. A creativity mantra might be something like the following:

- "Be a Fruit Loop in a bowl of Cheerios" (unattributed; sometimes cited as, "Be a Fruit Loop in a world full of Cheerios").
- "Think different" (a trademarked motto formerly used by Apple Computers).
- "Rather than seeing things as they are and asking 'Why?' we dream things that never were and ask 'Why not?'" (Adapted from a common saying of Robert Kennedy, who was, in turn, adapting a line from George Bernard Shaw's play *Back to Methuselah*. Ironically, Shaw attributes the line to the serpent in the Garden of Eden [Shaw 2011, 5]).
- "If you're not prepared to be wrong, you'll never come up with anything original" (Robinson and Aronica 2010, 15).
- "In order to have great ideas, you must first have many ideas" (adapted from a statement by Linus Pauling [Crick 1996]).
- *First, Break All the Rules* (title of a book by Marcus Buckingham and Curt Coffman, 1999).
- *What Got You Here Won't Get You There* (title of a book by Marshall Goldsmith, 2007).

At this point, some readers may object: "This is just what I was afraid of. All this talk about mindful leadership is just too squishy and 'New Age' for me. Leading a college or university needs something more profound than a few slogans or mottos." If you find yourself agreeing with these sentiments, just remember what the goal of mindful academic leadership is supposed to be: restoring our awareness to what's really happening and the things that are truly important for the success of our programs. You can't get more practical and down-to-earth than that.

Some academic leaders fixate on data and metrics, while others don't care enough about these things. Some see their role exclusively as dealing with people, while others view people as an unwelcome interference in their "real work." What mindful academic leadership offers is a way of providing balance to a job that's about both data and people, both metrics and conflicts.

If you find yourself objecting too strongly to an observation that some leaders find mottos useful devices to redirect their awareness to creativity (the development of new ideas) and innovation (the implementation of new ideas) when they become preoccupied with mere problem solving, it may be time to ask yourself what's so distasteful about this idea. It may well be defensiveness about what you perceive as your own lack of creativity or good interpersonal skills.

If the concept of using affirmations and creativity mottos doesn't appeal to you, don't use it. *Consider* it and have a good reason why you don't find it practical, but don't feel that you have to adopt it simply because this book or any other resources or people recommend it. There are plenty of other mindful leadership strategies in this book that may be more suitable for you.

But do keep in mind one thing before you dismiss this notion entirely: In workshops on this topic, the very people who object most strongly to the idea that meaningful mantras can help make leaders more creative are the ones who could benefit from this strategy the most. Typically, they're so caught up in data and information that they've lost sight of the living, breathing students, faculty members, and other administrators whose hopes and dreams are supposedly reflected in those data.

It's also important to realize that mantras, mottos, and slogans aren't the sum total of mindful academic leadership. Assuming that they are is rather like thinking that an alarm clock is the sum total of getting ready for work in the morning.

What the alarm clock does is wake us up and remind us of what we're supposed to be doing. A leadership or creativity mantra does exactly the same thing. It "wakes us up" when our attention has been distracted by all the minor decisions and petty squabbles we must deal with as administrators and redirects our attention toward "getting ready" for the activities that we say are important for the success of our programs. A mantra, slogan, or affirmation is, in short, a tool. It isn't the entire task.

MEETING MINDFULLY WITH MANTRAS

Like the other approaches to mindful academic leadership that we considered, mantras can also help us run meetings more effectively. Often when we say we're not satisfied with the time we spend in a meeting, it's because the reason for the group to assemble either wasn't clear to begin with or became diluted by all the separate goals or private agendas of those in attendance.

A meeting mantra—basically a single word or short phrase that serves as a mini-mission statement for the group—can be helpful in restoring people's awareness to their fundamental reason for getting together. Like the leadership touchstones that we considered earlier, a meeting mantra focuses attention and restores people's mindfulness of their common purpose. A meeting mantra doesn't need to be as condensed or focused as a mantra someone might use for a meditation exercise. In many cases, a common goal or a values touchstone is all that's needed.

For example, a curriculum committee might use a mantra like "Maximum student engagement in every course" as a way of reminding itself to look beyond content alone to consider the complete student experience in every course and program it considers. A search committee might adopt John C. Maxwell's Law of Magnetism—"Who you are is who you attract" (Maxwell 2010, 103–12)—to make sure that the members of the committee are aware that every phrase in a position announcement, every question they ask, and every e-mail or letter they send reflects on the values of the institution and program. An institutional review board (IRB) might choose the three core principles of the Belmont Report—"Respect for persons. Beneficence. And justice."—as its mantra every time it reviews a proposal (National Commission for the Protection of Human Subjects of Biomedical and Behavioral Research 1979).

Then, when discussions on the committee start to become sidetracked (and committee discussions in higher education almost always become sidetracked at some point), any member of the group can cite the mantra as a way of returning the attention of the committee to its primary goal. A meeting mantra thus works in much the same way as any of the other mindfulness techniques that we've explored: It gently guides people's attention back to the concerns of the present moment when, as will inevitably occur from time to time, they become distracted by other issues and lose sight of their main goal. A meeting mantra can also be used as part of an orientation for new members, indicating what the group's fundamental purpose is and how it goes about making its most important decisions.

FINAL REMARKS ON THE ROLE OF MANTRAS IN LEADERSHIP

There's one more aspect of mantras that academic leaders are wise to remember: Their titles and positions often serve as mantras for other people. Once we assume a formal position as an academic leader, even casual remarks we might make assume a different level of significance for many people. It's no longer "Bob said this" or "Jennifer believes that," but "The *dean* thinks we ought to . . ." or "The *provost* is considering . . ." If a mantra is, in certain ways, a word of power, then we have to remember that our titles have power even if we don't think of ourselves as particularly powerful or intimidating people.

The titles of academic leaders become mantras for those we work with in several different ways:

- *Matters of speculation.* If, at a meeting, a member of the faculty or staff says something along the lines of "I wonder what would happen if we just eliminated that program entirely," the remark will likely be regarded as nothing more than an exercise in thinking aloud. Some people may object. Others may express support for the idea. But no one will assume that the statement represents a major new policy initiative. Yet the result is likely to be quite different if an administrator utters those same words. At the very least, there will be those who conclude that the chair (or dean, provost, or president) has with those very words *proposed* the elimination of that program.
- *Matters of language and tone.* When a member of the faculty or staff criticizes a colleague, the object of those remarks may well take offense but could also view that criticism as a helpful idea or the advice of a concerned mentor. But as soon as you add the force of an administrator's title to criticism of someone who reports to that person, those words have a completely different effect. A mild suggestion may be regarded as a severe reprimand, casual advice about how to improve in the future may have a devastating effect on morale, and a general recommendation to do better in the future may come across as far more harsh than it was intended.
- *Matters of documentation.* This impact of speculation, language, and tone is multiplied many times when an academic leader's comments are made in writing. Documents live on long after the writer leaves his or her position. Memos remain in files. E-mail messages are archived. Even personal notes must sometimes be retained if they relate to ongoing concerns or important decisions. For this reason, a critical remark about an employee can cause problems years after it is written. The result is that administrators must sometimes make difficult choices about which documents to retain when a baseless accusation has been made against a member of the faculty or

staff. Does the academic leader file all of his or her notes in order to clarify the person's innocence if the question ever arises in the future? Or would it be more damaging to retain a record of an unjustified accusation since sometimes even those charges, groundless though they may be, can harm the employee's credibility?

- *Matters of association.* The organizations you belong to also become more highly scrutinized once you hold a leadership position. Your clubs and pastimes become reflections, not just of yourself, but also of the institution and the people you serve. When a president is a member of a country club that doesn't allow (or at least discourages) women and minorities from becoming members, that lapse in judgment is taken as a failure in judgment by the college or university as a whole. Moreover, our leadership titles may even have an effect on our casual associations. A small group of faculty members who get together for drinks or dinner on a regular basis seems harmless enough; these types of friendships can even be admirable if they help improve morale and increase job satisfaction. But a small, select group of faculty members who meet regularly for dinner or drinks with their chair, dean, or provost is likely to draw criticism and be viewed as a clique or, even worse, conspiracy. In a similar way, when a faculty member's friend receives a promotion or an unanticipated bonus, there is great cause for celebration. But when the close friend of an administrator receives a promotion or unplanned bonus, the suspicion may arise that more than merit was involved in that decision. It's not that you have to break off the relationships you have with members of the faculty and staff when you become their supervisor, but you do have to be aware of how the power of your title will affect how others view that friendship (Buller 2010).

In short, the powerful *constructive* effect that mantras can have in reminding us of our leadership principles and priorities can also be undermined by the powerful *destructive* effect that our positions and titles can produce when we're careless.

Mindful academic leaders aren't just mindful of their own goals and values; they're also mindful of how others may view their words and actions because of the positions of responsibility they hold.

KEY POINTS FROM CHAPTER 4

- Mantra mindfulness is concerned with awareness of the present moment or specific ideas through the use of specific words, phrases, or sounds.
- A meaningless mantra can be used in very much the same way as the breath is used in shamatha approaches and sensations are used in vipassana

approaches: to preserve the practitioner's awareness of experience as it occurs.
- A meaningful mantra can be used to preserve the awareness of either an individual practitioner or an entire group of a key value, goal, or purpose.
- Affirmations are, in many ways, just forms of meaningful mantras.
- Meaningful mantras are useful tools for achieving leadership goals that are more difficult to achieve through other mindfulness strategies. For example, meaningful mantras can help groups increase their creativity and encourage leaders to become more assertive and energized rather than more relaxed and tranquil.

EXERCISES TO COMPLETE BEFORE PROCEEDING TO CHAPTER 5

1. If you find yourself getting bored by the technique of meditating on meaningless mantras described in this chapter, you can vary it a bit by trying one or more of the following alterations:
   - Reverse the approach to breathing that you've been using. In other words, if you've been reciting your mantra as you inhale or exhale, experiment with using your mantra independently of your breathing pattern.
   - Sync the mantra with your in-breath or your out-breath if you've been reciting your mantra without regard to the way you breathe.
2. Similarly, if you'd like some variation in the technique of meditating on meaningful mantras described in this chapter, here are a couple of possibilities:
   - Experiment with meditating on the word *in* as you inhale and *out* as you exhale.
   - Let your own mantra emerge spontaneously by sitting in quiet contemplation until some word seems to "bubble up" from your subconscious. Use that word for your meditation session that day.
3. One of the drawbacks to using slogans or mottos as leadership mantras is that they begin to feel hackneyed and superficial through constant repetition. Some academic leaders thus prefer to choose a different saying each term or academic year and discuss it among the faculty and staff as their "Charge of the Year" or "Charge of the Term." An added advantage to this approach is that it enables the development of a leadership mantra that is singularly well suited to an area's needs at the moment. If you were to select a leadership mantra that best summarizes what would best serve your area at this stage in its development, what would it be?

REFERENCES

Adams, S. 2013. *How to Fail at Almost Everything and Still Win Big: Kind of the Story of My Life.* New York: Portfolio/Penguin.
Al-Mazrouei, M. M., (producer), and T. Taylor, T. (director). 2011. *The Help* [motion picture]. United States: Dreamworks.
Benson, H. 1975. *The Relaxation Response.* New York: Morrow.
Buckingham, M., and C. Coffman. 1999. *First, Break All the Rules: What the World's Greatest Managers Do Differently.* New York: Simon & Schuster.
Buller, J. L. 2010. "The Authority and Responsibility of the Title." *Academic Leader* 26, no. 3 (March): 4–5.
Carrington, P. 1998. *The Book of Meditation: The Complete Guide to Modern Meditation.* Boston: Element.
Coelho, P. (@paolocoelho). 2017. "Be a Good Person, But Don't Waste Your Time Trying to Prove It [tweet]." Twitter, July 13, 2017. https://twitter.com/paulocoelho/status/885472638981853193.
Crick, F. 1996. *The Impact of Linus Pauling on Molecular Biology* [lecture]. Retrieved from http://scarc.library.oregonstate.edu/events/1995paulingconference/video-s1-2-crick.html.
Franken, A., and M. Beattie. 1992. *I'm Good Enough, I'm Smart Enough, and Doggone It, People Like Me! Daily Affirmations by Stuart Smalley.* New York: Dell.
Goldsmith, M. 2007. *What Got You Here Won't Get You There: How Successful People Become Even More Successful!* New York: Hyperion.
Maharishi Foundation. 2017. Home. *Transcendental Meditation: The Technique for Inner Peace and Wellness.* Retrieved from http://www.tm.org/?leadsource=CRM1718&gclid=CPKj0u_g9NQCFciLswodbRYM8Q.
Maxwell, J. C. 2010. *The 21 Irrefutable Laws of Leadership: Follow Them and People Will Follow You.* Nashville: Thomas Nelson.
National Commission for the Protection of Human Subjects of Biomedical and Behavioral Research. 1979. "The Belmont Report." *Office for Human Research Protections*, April 18, 1979. Retrieved from https://www.hhs.gov/ohrp/regulations-and-policy/belmont-report/index.html.
Oliver, D. A. 2014. *Mantra Leadership: Don't Become the Emperor with No Clothes!* Bloomington, IN: Xlibris.
Robinson, K., and L. Aronica. 2010. *The Element: How Finding Your Passion Changes Everything.* London, UK: Penguin.
Shaw, B. 2011. *Back to Methuselah.* Overland Park, KS: Digireads/Neeland.

RESOURCES

Kruse, K. 2017. "Become an Amazing Leader with a Simple Mantra." *Forbes*, June 14, 2017. Retrieved from https://www.forbes.com/sites/kevinkruse/2017/06/14/become-an-amazing-leader-with-a-simple-mantra/#381e8faf591f.

Ryan, M. J. 2016. *Habit Changers: 81 Game-Changing Mantras to Mindfully Realize Your Goals.* New York: Crown Business.

Walter, E. 2014. "Mantras That Guide Thriving Organizations." *Forbes*, September 24, 2014. Retrieved from https://www.forbes.com/sites/ekaterinawalter/2014/09/24/mantras-that-guide-thriving-organizations/#c4d3ddb429c5.

Chapter 5

Metta

Expanding Compassion

With our discussion of the mantra approach to mindfulness, we shifted from a concern for simple awareness of the present moment to a concern for being aware of a specific idea or value in the present moment. As we move to the last of the four main approaches to mindfulness that we'll consider—meditative and non-meditative approaches to metta—that shift will continue. Metta mindfulness is an approach in which what we remain aware of is both how we want to treat others and the type of world we want to create by our actions.

The word *maitrī* (Sanskrit) or *mettā* (its Pali equivalent) means any and all of the following: benevolence, kindness, loving-kindness, friendliness, amity, friendship, goodwill, and active interest in others. Its key concept is a desire for others to be well, safe, and happy.

Although that may have been the implicit goal of the other types of mindfulness that we've considered, with metta mindfulness, the happiness of others becomes our *explicit* goal. As such, it's an excellent complement to a mindfulness practice that begins in increasing our general awareness of the world but only reaches its fruition when we're fully aware of how we want to affect the world.

METTA MEDITATION

A meditative approach to metta begins with the identification of three different people who will become your object of thought and concern throughout the exercise:

1. Someone you care deeply about. This person should be someone for whom you find it very easy to be reminded of positive feelings, someone whose welfare is an almost constant concern for you.
2. Someone you know or are acquainted with but have no real feelings about one way or the other. This person might be someone you encounter at work and perhaps say good morning to a few times a week but don't otherwise interact with and for whom you don't have any strong feelings of either affection or dislike. It's okay to identify this person as "the guard at the front desk" or "the student who delivers our mail" if you don't know his or her name.
3. Someone who is a difficult person for you. This person should be someone with whom you have had a troubled past, you actively dislike, or over whom you feel pain or regret whenever you think of the person.

Next, two more parties need to be added to this list:

4. Yourself.
5. Everyone in the world (or, if you prefer, all living creatures).

Although you'll quickly find that the cycle of metta meditation that we'll describe becomes almost second nature, people who are just starting this approach sometimes like to keep that list as well as the following instructions in front of them for the first few sessions. In that way, if their thoughts wander, they don't increase their sense of distraction by having to reconstruct their list and recall the steps of the procedure. Metta meditation can look a bit complicated, but it's actually quite easy once you've tried it a few times.

Here are the steps involved:

1. Complete the standard meditation preparation as described in chapter 2.
2. Pause for a moment to set aside your normal work and activities, focusing your attention on the fact that you're about to meditate. If it helps to do so, practice the shamatha technique for several breaths until you feel calm and prepared to begin the exercise.
3. Set a timer for five minutes.
4. Begin with the first person on your list, the person you care deeply about. For the ease of reference, let's call this person Alicia. Slowly and thoughtfully, recite the following thoughts in your mind: "May Alicia be happy. May Alicia be healthy. May Alicia be safe. May Alicia be free from care."
5. Pause slightly.
6. Then go on to the second person on your list, the person you have no feelings about one way or the other. Since you may not even know this

person's name, in our example, we'll call this person "our parking attendant." Slowly and thoughtfully, recite the following thoughts in your mind: "May our parking attendant be happy. May our parking attendant be healthy. May our parking attendant be safe. May our parking attendant be free from care."
7. Pause slightly.
8. Then continue through your list, thinking these same four thoughts about the person with whom you've had difficulty, yourself, and everyone in the world or all living creatures.
9. When you've completed thinking the four kind thoughts about everyone or all living things, return to the first person on your list and start all over again.
10. Whenever you realize that your attention has wandered off and that you've been thinking of things other than these kind thoughts, simply pick up where you left off (if you can recall) or start over again at the top of your list.
11. Continue this process until the timer goes off.

Reviewing the Experience

After experimenting with the metta style of meditation, you may wonder why the people you're asked to think about proceed in the order indicated. Why, in particular, are you asked to think generous thoughts about someone with whom you've had some difficulties before you extend these thoughts to yourself? The answer to this question is that the sequence is based on how easy most people find it to be honestly and seriously compassionate about each person or group. You start with someone you already care about. That's easy. You certainly wish this person well. In fact, you probably think kind and loving thoughts about this person several times a day anyway.

Moving to a person you are familiar with but don't have strong feelings about one way or the other is a fairly small step. You know that you don't really *dis*like that person, so wishing that person well doesn't seem too hard. Then, making the transition to thinking those same thoughts about someone you *do* dislike—or at least have had some problems with in the past—seems a natural progression. After all, we know that we're not supposed to wish harm upon those we don't care for, so moving from a neutral person to what we might call a negative person in our lives strikes us as ethical and appropriate.

But here's the interesting phenomenon about metta meditation: Most people find it easier to think positive thoughts about a person they don't like than to think those same thoughts about themselves. "Only narcissists and sociopaths wish themselves well all the time," we may think (even if we don't articulate that thought in precisely those words). It can be extremely difficult for many people to dive immediately into a meditative process in which they devote time to thinking that they *deserve* generosity from themselves.

But wishing ourselves well somehow becomes a bit easier when we've just thought positively about someone who has been a problem for us. Perhaps it's because we feel that, having just demonstrated virtue in loving our enemies, we're now entitled to a little bit of self-love. Or perhaps it's because we feel that there's a certain justice to the progression we've just made: We certainly didn't put our own needs first; in fact, we even put the needs of near strangers and people we dislike before our own.

And even if we still do harbor some reluctance to feeling that we merit those few moments of self-absorption, the final step in the series follows immediately. We wish health, safety, and other good things to *everyone*, and "everyone" includes us, right?

So, the way in which we proceed through these thoughts has an important purpose. It reminds us to demonstrate compassion, not merely to those who are already dear to us, but to others as well. And it reminds us that we have to demonstrate compassion toward ourselves, too. The stresses and challenges of academic leadership are so great that we need to be a little kind to ourselves from time to time. After all, there are days when, if we're not generous to ourselves, no one else will be either.

Moreover, a little bit of self-compassion is necessary for us to be truly effective as academic leaders. The unskillful things we do at work don't occur because we have negative or undesirable thoughts and feelings. Such thoughts or feelings are inevitable. Everybody has them.

Instead, we do unskillful things because we get "hooked" by these thoughts and feelings, like fish caught on a line. Getting hooked by a negative or undesirable thought can happen in one of two ways. First, we can buy into these thoughts and feelings, treating them like facts rather than as artifacts of our minds. We know we're getting hooked in this way when we start to revert to thoughts like the following:

- "It was just the same at my last job. Things went well for a while, and then I began to get in over my head. I'm just no good at this."
- "Sooner or later people are going to see what a fraud I am. Some days I can't understand how I even made it this far."
- "I'm not going to take on yet another new project. I've been burned before. Getting involved just isn't worth it."

Second, and somewhat paradoxically, we can get hooked by thoughts and feelings by the very process of trying to rationalize them away. The process then becomes something like the following:

- "I shouldn't be having thoughts like this. My whole problem is that I keep beating myself up."
- "I've just got to suck it up, get over myself, and forget about all this negativity."
- "Why am I wallowing in these thoughts and feelings? Who do I think I am that I believe life should be easier than it is?"

In both cases, we're caught up in one particular set of thoughts and feelings—either because we start wallowing in them or because we're devoting so much energy to trying to block them out—with the result that we become less mindful of our current experience and of all the good things that people (even the people with whom we've had some difficulty) are doing all around us. Metta meditation reminds us that, just as the problematic people in our lives aren't perfect, we aren't either. But that's okay. We're all trying to do what's best. It's just that sometimes we don't meet the high expectations we set for ourselves.

Progressing with Metta Meditation

As you continue with metta meditation, you may find your "cast of characters" is changing over time. After thinking generous thoughts about the person toward whom you were initially indifferent, you may discover that you want to get to know that person a little better, learn his or her name if you don't know it already, and begin regarding that person more as a friend than a mere acquaintance. Similarly, after a number of positive thoughts about the person you once disliked, you may find your feelings about that person softening and becoming a bit more sympathetic.

All of that is great. You've transformed a stranger into a friend, and the number of difficult people in your life has decreased by one. That's progress, and it involved nothing more than thinking a few thoughts in a specific order.

Some people also like to combine shamatha and metta techniques into a single hybrid approach. To do this, they think "May So-and-so be happy," as they inhale, "May So-and-so be healthy," as they exhale, "May So-and-so be safe," on the next in-breath, and "May So-and-so be free from care," on the next out-breath.

Then they proceed to the next person on their list. You might discover that this technique makes it much easier for you to keep your mind from wandering, grounding you as it does in both awareness of the present moment and reminding you that this present moment is an excellent time to start showing other people a higher degree of kindness.

NON-MEDITATIVE APPROACHES TO METTA

Even people who are reluctant to try other approaches to meditation sometimes find that the metta technique works well for them. It doesn't seem like other types of meditation. Aside from the term *metta* itself, there's no unusual vocabulary. (And if even that term bothers you, you can just think of it as a *kindness exercise*.) It doesn't require any particular posture or special equipment. You don't even have to be aware of your breath if you don't want to be. It's simply a series of positive thoughts about various people.

Nevertheless, for those who still prefer approaches to mindfulness that don't require any meditation whatsoever, there are still a number of techniques that produce much the same result as the technique described above but don't involve meditation.

The first of these techniques is David J. Pollay's Law of the Garbage Truck. Pollay relates that he was once in New York, heading to Grand Central Station in a cab. A car suddenly pulled out in front of them, causing the cab driver to have to brake suddenly and bring the car to a stop within a few centimeters of the car that had cut them off. The driver of that car, who had almost caused the accident, then proceeded to curse the cab driver, threw him an obscene gesture, and prepared to drive away. Pollay was certain that the cab driver's response was going to be equal anger, but he merely smiled, waved at the other driver, and let him proceed.

Pollay was dumbfounded by the cab driver's reaction and asked him what he was thinking. The cab driver replied,

> Many people are like garbage trucks. They run around full of garbage, full of frustration, full of anger, and full of disappointment. As their garbage piles up, they look for a place to dump it. And if you let them, they'll dump it on you. So when someone wants to dump on you, don't take it personally. Just smile, wave, wish them well, and move on. Believe me, you'll be happier. (Pollay 2011, 10)

The type of reaction Pollay's cab driver had is sometimes referred to as *strategic non-response*. It involves the conscious decision that the best response in a given situation is no response at all, at least no hostile, angry, or negative response.

Pollay's Law of the Garbage Truck recognizes that we all carry around with us a certain amount of hurt and frustration. But for some people, that hurt and frustration reaches the point where it's about to spill over, and the person feels that he or she needs to "dump" that pain onto someone else. The Law of the Garbage Truck contains the recognition that, merely because someone wants to *give* you anger and negativity, it doesn't mean that you have to *receive* their anger and negativity. To put the matter as briefly as possible, *if someone keeps pushing your buttons, why not just disconnect the buttons?*

In *A Toolkit for College Professors* (2015), the authors introduce the concepts of positive and negative default (Buller and Cipriano 2015, 64–68). Negative default begins with the assumption that most people are basically evil, lazy, incompetent, or all three. When someone does something wrong, people whose default mindset is negative assume that the person who made the error was stupid, trying to do harm, or out to get them for some reason.

Positive default begins with the assumption that most people are usually trying to do things right, even though they may not always live up to their own expectations. Those whose default mindset is positive assume that, when someone does something wrong, he or she was *trying* to do something right; it's just that he or she didn't *get* it right. In brief, when someone with negative default asks, "What's wrong with you?" it sounds like an accusation. When someone with positive default asks, "What's wrong with you?" it sounds like an expression of concern.

In academic leadership, concepts like the Law of the Garbage Truck or strategic non-response harmonize well with a perspective of positive default. Because of the constant pressures and deadlines of academic work—those short timetables faculty members have to achieve tenure, the never-ending demand that college professors publish in top-tier journals and receive external funding for their research, and the stresses people are under from the requirements imposed by governing boards that colleges and universities meet performance targets in terms of retention, graduation rates, job placement, and so on—mean that most of the people we interact with are carrying around with them a heavy load of frustration, anxiety, and anger at the bureaucracy that makes a hard job even harder.

It's no wonder that members of the faculty and staff alike are so often tense and occasionally even explode, directing their venom at the nearest available symbols of "the system," which happen to be us as academic leaders. We can respond negatively, thus adding fuel to an already blazing fire, or we can act with compassion and understanding, realizing that the vast majority of people are trying to do what's best in an environment that doesn't always make that task easy.

One way of viewing this first technique of approaching metta from a non-meditative perspective is to engage in what we might call *Bless and Release*. When we find ourselves on the receiving end of someone's rancor, we simply—like David Pollay's taxi driver—wish them well and send them on their way.

The heat of the moment is rarely the best time to discuss the issues that are bothering that person. Demonstrating generosity toward the person when he or she is upset, and then working constructively to make his or her situation better when things are calmer helps us be mindful of our own desire to improve the experience of our stakeholders and may lead to a reduction in the load of "garbage" that we ourselves bear.

Rewrite the Movie

The story about David Pollay's taxi driver may remind us of another famous character who drove a cab in New York: Travis Bickle, portrayed by Robert De Niro in Martin Scorsese's 1976 film *Taxi Driver*. Bickle's most famous quote from the movie is "You talkin' to me? You talkin' to me? You talkin' to *me*? Then who the hell else are you talking . . . you talking to me? Well I'm the only one here. Who . . . do you think you're talking to?" (Phillips, Phillips, and Scorsese 1976). Clearly, Travis Bickle is not the sort of person who would practice bless and release, much less engage in any form of meditation.

Many people adore the movie *Taxi Driver* because of its exploration of the limits to free will, its gritty realism, and its depiction of how routine exposure to violence can result in lasting psychological trauma. Others, however, condemn the movie for appearing to revel in the violence it supposedly condemns, its reduction of characters to stereotypes, and its ambiguous ending.

Let's conduct a brief thought experiment and suppose for a moment that you fall into the latter category. You don't just dislike the movie *Taxi Driver*; you absolutely hate it. You regard it as one of the worst movies ever made, and you find enduring even a few minutes of it to be a form of severe torture.

If that were the case, you wouldn't watch *Taxi Driver* repeatedly, would you? You wouldn't put the movie on and force yourself to watch it every time you found that it was available. You would simply conclude that viewing that particular movie was an unpleasant experience and choose instead to devote your leisure time to forms of entertainment that were more to your taste.

The point of the thought experiment is this: If you wouldn't repeatedly watch a movie you hated, why would you keep doing so for all those angry or negative thoughts you keep replaying in your mind? For many of us, our thoughts seem to be on an endless loop of self-recrimination, self-criticism, and finding others to blame when we're not in the mood to blame ourselves.

Elisha Goldstein, the cofounder of the Center for Mindful Living in West Los Angeles, calls these thoughts "the movies in our minds" and has some simple but highly effective advice about how to deal with them: Just rewrite the movie (Goldstein 2013, 63–70). You can decide that you're tired of watching the same old "film" (which you never particularly enjoyed anyway) and that you'd prefer something a little more to your taste. Maybe the movie you write will end up being a little less *Taxi Driver* and a little more *It's a Wonderful Life* (Capra 1946).

The metta approach to mindfulness reminds us that, just as we need to overcome our frustration with others and forgive them for the mistakes that they make, we also need to forgive ourselves. That can be difficult because, as Roy Baumeister of Florida State University and others discovered in a study of what we tend to remember most vividly, our memories of painful moments usually last longer and affect us more than our memories of our successes.

> The greater power of bad events over good ones is found in everyday events. . . . Bad emotions . . . and bad feedback have more impact than good ones, and bad information is processed more thoroughly than good. . . . Bad impressions and bad stereotypes are quicker to form and more resistant to [change] than good ones. (Baumeister, Bratslavsky, and Finkenauer 2001, 323)

In addition, the work done by the social psychologist Dan Gilbert of Harvard University helps explain why this phenomenon occurs. Every time we recall an unpleasant event, we're not just reviewing an impression it made on us; we're actually recreating the event, reliving it in some ways, and revising it so that it becomes more vivid and more powerful over time. As Gilbert describes this process,

> Remembering an experience feels a lot like opening a drawer and retrieving a story that was filed away on the day it was written, but . . . that feeling is one of our brain's most sophisticated illusions. Memory is not a dutiful scribe that keeps a complete transcript of our experiences, but a sophisticated editor that clips and saves key elements to rewrite the story each time we ask to reread it. (Gilbert 2006, 217–18)

Fortunately, that bad news also contains the germ of some good news: If we spontaneously rewrite our memories in an unconscious manner, we can equally well rewrite our memories in a conscious manner so that they no longer affect us in negative or destructive ways.

As Elisha Goldstein said, we're able to rewrite the "movies in our minds" so that we're no longer the failure, loser, or incompetent that we remember but rather just a person who was trying to do the best he or she could at the time and didn't prove to be successful at *that* attempt. But that attempt also does not define who we are for the future. What was once a memory of disappointment and failure can be rewritten as a story of learning from a difficult experience. We're no longer the victims of the story; we're the heroes.

Using this same approach, we can recast all the other characters in our mental movies as well. Instead of pigeonholing the people we work with as the whiner, the idiot, and the backstabber, we can create new mental roles for them, which will probably affect how we interact with them and our attitudes about them. In some cases, we may notice that they actually begin to grow into the new roles in which we've cast them. More often, however, we'll merely find ourselves acting more generously and humanely because we've now recast our mental movies to have more heroes than villains.

Cognitive Diffusion

Another non-meditative technique we can use for gaining perspective on the negative thoughts we have about ourselves or others is cognitive diffusion. It begins with recognizing the thought that's causing us to act in unskillful ways. That thought might be about someone else ("Jean is such a complainer") or about our own mistakes and failings ("I'm lazy, overweight, and uncreative"). As you think these thoughts, you're likely to behave in ungenerous ways—or at least be tempted to do so. You'll start avoiding Jean and give up trying for that promotion because you think you could never deserve it. With cognitive diffusion, you don't prevent yourself from thinking those thoughts, but you add two steps to the process that "diffuses" their impact.

The first step is to add the phrase "I'm having the thought that . . ." in front of whatever notion it was that you've identified as problematic. For example, the next time you find yourself annoyed with Jean because of all her gripes, you start to think, "I'm having the thought that Jean is such a complainer."

Then you do something that may seem counterintuitive: Instead of resisting or avoiding the thought, you consciously and intentionally *yield to it*, as long as you make sure to prefix it with "I'm having the thought that . . ." You then indulge in this reflection for a minute or two. That's all the time that it takes.

In fact, you'll notice that if you set a timer for two minutes and force yourself to engage in these thoughts until the timer goes off, the two minutes will seem very long indeed. At the end of this short reflection, you'll probably discover that you're feeling less negative about Jean or yourself than you were before. You managed to shift from *having* a feeling to *being aware* of that feeling.

And that means that you're now ready for the second step: Add the phrase "I'm aware that . . ." to the previous sentence and give in to this new thought for a minute or two. So, in our examples, you'll now be thinking, "I'm aware that I'm having the thought that Jean is such a complainer," or, "I'm aware that I'm having the thought that I'm lazy, overweight, and uncreative." By doing so, you diffuse your negative emotions once again, gaining even greater distance from them and seeing them more clearly for what they are: mere expressions of feelings, not statements of reality.

The whole process takes less than five minutes and moves you systematically from a negative emotion to objective analysis of that emotion. The result is that you now have a choice. You can keep avoiding Jean if that seems like the most productive strategy, or you can start to see her positive contributions. You can make only a halfhearted effort to get that promotion, if that's what you really want to do, or you can act more skillfully, make your best case for the position, and increase the likelihood that you'll be seriously considered for it.

Cognitive diffusion works particularly well for academic leaders because our training has prepared us to be as objective as possible when examining evidence within our chosen disciplines. By engaging in the two steps of this process, we "switch off" our tendencies to respond emotionally to whatever it is that's bothering us and "switch on" our intellectual, analytical capacities.

You may have witnessed a similar phenomenon if, during an encounter with someone who was angry, you happened to ask for a specific piece of information, like the person's phone number or e-mail address. Many times in these situations, the person's demeanor shifts noticeably as they "switch off" their angry, emotional modes and "switch on" their objective, information retrieval modes. When we practice cognitive diffusion, we engage in that same type of transition, the only difference being that we're now conversing with ourselves instead of with someone else.

Although it's such a simple technique, cognitive diffusion combines several important aspects of mindful academic leadership. It directs our awareness to the present moment, permitting us to select our most skillful option rather than responding mindlessly. And it urges us to lean into our negative thoughts and feelings about ourselves or others rather than suppressing them.

By embracing these thoughts and feelings in a conscious, intentional manner, we deprive them of any power they might have over us. Our current practice of indulging those notions and emotions simply empowers them, increasing the chances that our actions will be ungenerous, perhaps even cruel.

Cognitive Distancing

The final non-meditative technique for increasing metta that we'll consider is likely to strike some readers as a bit silly. But from personal experience as well as the reports of those who have tried it, it can be almost instantaneous in its ability to break down unkind thoughts and emotions and restore our control over difficult situations.

The technique is quite simple: *When you find yourself repeatedly thinking an ungenerous thought about yourself or others, imagine that same sentiment spoken in a ridiculous cartoon voice.* It's one thing to beat yourself up over and over again with the thought that you're just not good enough and never will be, and it's something quite different to imagine those words coming out of the mouth of Daffy Duck, Elmer Fudd, or some other comic character.

In a similar way, the contempt you feel for your colleague Roger is likely to dissipate when you hear yourself think, "Here come's that back-stabbing Roger again," not in your own voice, but in the voice of Bart Simpson or Marvin the Martian.

In fact, if you're having negative thoughts that you find particularly disruptive to your goals of kindly and benevolent leadership, there's even software available that can help you with this kind of cognitive distancing. Celebrity Voice Changer, a smartphone app produced by Hays Off Apps, can alter any statement you record so that it sounds like Elmo, Obi-Wan Kenobi, Arnold Schwarzenegger, Donald Trump, Hillary Clinton, a variety of fairy princesses, and a large assortment of other cartoon characters, political figures, and media personalities. Voice Changer Plus, by Arf Software Inc., allows you to alter your voice so that what you say sounds as though it were affected by helium, uttered by a robot, said extremely fast or slow, and so on.

Even our least charitable thoughts lose some of their power over us when they sound ridiculous. Cognitive distancing is thus a technique that allows us to hear how ridiculous these unkind thoughts are by presenting our own words to us stripped of the impact we give them when we hear them in our own voices.

METTA-BASED LEADERSHIP

Taking a kinder, more generous perspective toward yourself and others may make you a better person. But can we seriously claim that it also makes you a better leader? As a way of answering this question, the best place to begin is with the following observation by Janice Marturano, the founder and executive director of the Institute for Mindful Leadership:

> Being kind is not the same . . . as being polite or politically correct. Kindness comes from compassion, an authentic connection to others and the pains and joys they feel. . . . Compassion practice can also help us form a new relationship with those who are difficult with us. (Marturano 2015, 159)

In other words, metta-based leadership shouldn't be confused with merely being a popular or convivial leader. In the same way, it's not the same thing as just letting people do whatever it is they want to do.

Instead, what metta helps leaders do is see matters from the perspective of the various stakeholders they serve. It causes us to recognize that even those who end up doing something very wrong probably started out by doing something they thought was good. We can thus provide better guidance for our areas because we better understand how the people we work with and for see the world, what matters to them, and where their individual challenges and frustrations lie.

The way in which metta can shape our practice as academic leaders can be illustrated through a brief scenario. Imagine that three people who report to you spent most of an academic year preparing a grant proposal that ultimately did not get funded. Several other important activities either went undone or had to be assigned to your already overworked colleagues because of the time these three people spent on the proposal.

You offered repeatedly to help and gave the best suggestions that you could, but those who were working on the grant proposal ignored your advice. The advice you gave them included consulting with a program officer at the funding agency. They didn't do that, even though you're certain they would have received helpful insights. Nor did they take full advantage of the resources offered by your institution's division of research or consult previous grant applications that were successful.

When the grant proposal is rejected by the funding agency, and it's clear that the request never even made it past the first round of screening, your initial temptation is to say, "I told you so!" and punish the three grant writers somehow for wasting time and resources. But would that lead to the best possible outcome? It might be satisfying to vent your frustration in the short term, but acting in a punitive way still won't get your proposal funded or bring you back all the time that was lost in its development.

A fair question is "Were the three people actually *trying* to write a bad proposal?" They almost certainly weren't, so treating them as though they intentionally set out to waste time, harm the program, or burden their colleagues with extra work is likely to be misguided. What probably occurred is that they were actually trying to do what they thought was right; they simply missed that mark and wound up getting it wrong.

So, if we don't approach this situation from a perspective of negative default, how can we be more positive and generous in our approach while still demonstrating effective academic leadership? We can start by making the situation a learning experience and help the unsuccessful grant writers do a better job next time. We can explore with them why they were so resistant to your advice and unwilling to consult with either the funding agency or the division of research.

Perhaps they had had so much success in submitting proposals in the past that they were overconfident in their abilities. That's an issue that can be addressed as a leadership challenge. You can explore with them what may have changed about the way in which proposals are evaluated since their last successful attempt, how different funding agencies may have vastly different criteria, and why an open teamwork model ("Let's all do this together") is usually more effective than the closed clique model ("We don't need you. We know what we're doing") that led them to failure.

Perhaps, too, it was a matter of group dynamics among the three grant writers that caused the problem. In a phenomenon known as the *Abilene Paradox*, groupthink or the suggestion of one influential member of a group can cause a team to continue a strategy that most or even all the group members recognize as unsuccessful. The Abilene Paradox derives its name from an article written by the late professor of management at George Washington University, Jerry B. Harvey.

In the scenario suggested by Harvey, a family in Coleman, Texas, is playing dominoes on a hot afternoon. Because they're all so bored, the father mentions that they could drive to Abilene for dinner. One by one everyone agrees, and the family begins the long, dusty, uncomfortable ride to Abilene. When they get back home hours later, exhausted and annoyed by the foolish trip, they find out that no one in the family really *wanted* to go to Abilene. Each person merely thought that the others did and didn't want to be the person who ruined it for everyone else (Harvey 1974).

Departments, committees, and task forces sometimes get on their own "road to Abilene." They start proceeding in a certain direction—at times because no one has any better ideas and at other times because people don't want to object to an idea raised by one of their colleagues—and don't stop even when it's clear that that direction isn't getting them any closer to their destination.

As an academic leader, it isn't effective to punish people for acting that way. They didn't go in the wrong direction intentionally. They actually thought they were doing something right. A better approach is to work with the group compassionately and generously, analyzing what went wrong without unduly assigning blame, and to figure out how to work together more effectively in the future.

MEETING MINDFULLY WITH METTA

The type of understanding of and compassion for others that is derived from metta can also make you more effective at leading and even just attending meetings. Particularly for meetings that have a history of being contentious, go over in your mind all the likely attendees in advance.

Decide that you hope each person will be happy, healthy, safe, and free from care. Resolve that, for yourself at least, the upcoming meeting will be a "garbage holiday": No matter what frustrations, anger, and annoyance the people in attendance try to dump on you, you won't be collecting their "trash" this time. You'll mentally "rewrite the movie" of how you hope the meeting will go and do your best to make sure that your positive, more constructive "script" plays out.

A commonplace among receptionists and other people whose job requires them to receive a lot of phone calls is that it's always most effective to smile whenever answering the phone. The person placing the call can't see you (unless you're videoconferencing, of course), but he or she can "hear" the smile in your tone.

In a similar manner, you can prepare for meetings by smiling as you think about every person who will be there, the issues that you'll discuss, and the goals you hope to achieve. The members of the group may not yet be with you so that they can *see* your smile, but they very well may *hear* it in the tone you then take when the meeting finally occurs.

FINAL REMARKS ON METTA

Metta mindfulness helps us transform *enemy thinking* ("Baxter did that because he's out to get me") into more *sympathetic thinking* ("Baxter did that because we see things differently"), *troublemaker thinking* ("Janice acts that way because she's difficult to work with") into more *understanding thinking* ("Maybe if I get to know Janice better, I'll figure out why she acts that way"), and *obstacle thinking* ("We'll never get this passed; the faculty senate is just too politicized") into *opportunity thinking* ("Perhaps if we partner with the faculty senate on the proposal, we can form a united front"). It helps us recognize that most people are actually trying to do what's right most of the time, and so we can tap into this positive and constructive energy instead of becoming bogged down in negative and destructive conflict.

In our roles as academic leaders, metta mindfulness enables us to be at our most effective because it causes us to be assertive rather than aggressive. We're aggressive when we objectify others by treating them like obstacles to be cleared away or tools for the success of our initiatives rather than as genuine human beings. In its own way, aggression is just as manipulative as being calculating in achieving goals that may be important to us but harmful or useless to others. It occurs when we regard people as means to an end rather than as the end in themselves. Assertiveness, on the other hand, shows the people we work with respect by presenting our arguments clearly, listening to their concerns sincerely, and adjusting our ideas appropriately.

Finally, metta mindfulness improves our academic leadership by not exacerbating negativity needlessly. When someone annoys us or is rude to us, we recognize that he or she may be having a bad day or may simply be frustrated by the situation, not by us personally. Inherent in academic leadership is the fact that we represent the offices we hold and, at times, the bureaucracy of the institution itself. When people direct anger toward us, they're often not really angry at us but at "the dean," "the administration," or "the system."

Metta mindfulness helps us remember that we've found bureaucracy frustrating ourselves at times. And so, rather than heaping gasoline on the fire of people's bitterness when they're upset, we hope that they may be happy, healthy, safe, and free from care, and then we work together with them to solve the problem and make our program even better for the future.

KEY POINTS FROM CHAPTER 5

- Metta mindfulness is concerned, not simply with awareness itself, but with awareness of generous and benevolent feelings toward others.
- A common way of performing the metta approach to meditation is to think kind thoughts about people in our lives whom we like and others whom we don't like and to wish those people well.
- Many of the advantages of metta meditation can also be achieved by techniques like strategic non-response, cognitive diffusion, and cognitive distancing. We can also consciously rewrite the "movies" that we replay in our heads, those thoughts that occur to us over and over again almost against our wills.
- Metta mindfulness helps us become better leaders by seeing everyone we work with as fully three-dimensional people with their own perspectives, goals, and frustrations. It enables us to avoid treating people as tools to achieve our goals or as obstacles in our path and to understand better how they, like us, are usually trying to do their best in difficult circumstances.
- Meetings are often more productive when we practice the metta approach to mindfulness because it enables us to become less fixated on the goal of the meeting itself and more receptive to the needs of our partners in achieving that goal.

EXERCISES TO COMPLETE BEFORE PROCEEDING TO CHAPTER 6

1. If you find yourself getting bored by the metta meditation technique described in this chapter, you can vary it a bit by trying one or more of the following alterations:
    - You can direct kind and generous thoughts toward compass points ("May everyone to my north be happy, healthy, safe, and free from care. May everyone to my east . . . .") instead of toward specific people.
    - Rather than verbalizing compassionate thoughts about specific people, you can visualize them as happy and grateful for your concern.

- You can engage in metta meditation while walking, making one benevolent wish about someone with each step you take.
- You can include yourself with each wish, rephrasing your thoughts as, "Just as I want to be happy, so may [NAME OF PERSON] be happy. Just as I want to be healthy, so may [NAME OF PERSON] be healthy," and so on.
- You can experiment with some of the additional variations of metta meditation presented at Brown 2015.
- You can try the Tibetan meditative practice known as *tonglen* in which you wish benevolence toward others while expressing a willingness to absorb their sufferings yourself. Like other types of meditation, tonglen has many forms, but a common variation is to visualize yourself as sending forth positive feelings on each out breath ("May Dylan be happy") and absorbing suffering on each in-breath ("May I assume Dylan's unhappiness").

2. Similarly, if you want to try some variations of the non-meditative approaches to metta that were explained in this chapter, consider the following activities:
   - Identify a specific stakeholder group for each day of your workweek, such as faculty members on Monday, staff members on Tuesday, students on Wednesday, donors on Thursday, and everyone else on Friday. Then go out of your way to thank or praise someone in that stakeholder group at some point during that day. (See Buller 2013, 146–47.)
   - Whenever meeting a new person, mentally wish that person well as you shake his or her hand.
   - Consider some of what Maria Gonzalez calls her "mindfulness-in-action strategies," as presented in Gonzalez 2012, 172–73.

3. Now that you have read about the four different forms of meditation that we've discussed in this book, try the following:
   - Choose one of these forms to serve as the basis for a regular meditation practice. Resolve to practice it for ten or fifteen minutes a day. Remember that the consistency of your practice is far more important than its duration. So, even if you can only meditate for five minutes or so some days, perform the technique as long as you can, and don't skip a day.
   - If you have the time, conduct your own meditation retreat. Combine the four forms we've covered by practicing each of them for ten or fifteen minutes then proceeding to the next form. Many people find that the order in which these meditation techniques are presented in this book (shamatha first, then vipassana, mantra, and metta in turn) makes a logical progression. If more time remains, simply keep cycling through the techniques in that order for as long as you have available.

REFERENCES

Baumeister, B. F., E. Bratslavsky, and C. Finkenauer. 2001. "Bad Is Stronger Than Good." *Review of General Psychology* 5 (4): 323–70.

Brown, P. 2015. "Loving-Kindness (Metta) Meditation." *Buddhist Sangha of Bucks County*, March 27, 2015. Retrieved from http://buddhistsangha.com/2015/03/27/loving-kindness-metta-meditation/.

Buller, J. L. 2013. *Positive Academic Leadership: How to Stop Putting Out Fires and Start Making a Difference*. San Francisco: Jossey-Bass.

Buller, J. L., and R. E. Cipriano. 2015. *A Toolkit for College Professors*. Lanham, MD: Rowman & Littlefield.

Capra, F. (producer and director). 1946. *It's a Wonderful Life* [motion picture]. United States: RKO.

Gilbert, D. T. 2006. *Stumbling on Happiness*. New York: Knopf.

Goldstein, E. 2013. *The Now Effect: How a Mindful Moment Can Change the Rest of Your Life*. New York: Aria.

Gonzalez, M. 2012. *Mindful Leadership: The 9 Ways to Self-Awareness, Transforming Yourself, and Inspiring Others*. San Francisco: Jossey-Bass.

Harvey, J. B. 1974. "The Abilene Paradox: The Management of Agreement." *Organizational Dynamics* 3 (1): 63–80.

Marturano, J. 2015. *Finding the Space to Lead: A Practical Guide to Mindful Leadership*. New York: Bloomsbury Press.

Phillips, J., and M. Phillips (producers), and M. Scorsese (director). 1976. *Taxi Driver* [motion picture]. United States: Columbia.

Pollay, D. J. 2011. *Law of the Garbage Truck*. New York: Sterling.

RESOURCES

Gunaratana, H. 2017. *Loving-Kindness in Plain English: The Practice of Metta*. Somerville, MA: Wisdom Publications.

Kristeller, J. L., and T. Johnson. 2005, June 1. "Cultivating Loving Kindness: A Two-Stage Model of the Effects of Meditation on Empathy, Compassion, and Altruism." *Zygon: Journal of Religion and Science* 40 (2): 391–408.

Salzberg, S. 2008. *Loving-Kindness: The Revolutionary Art of Happiness*. Boston: Shambhala.

Salzberg, S. 2011. *Real Happiness: The Power of Meditation, a 28-Day Program*. New York: Workman.

Chapter 6

Organic, Positive, and Authentic Mindfulness

The last topic we need to consider is why mindful leadership is particularly important in higher education. That is to say, so many of the benefits that we've seen resulting from the approaches we've been exploring could apply to leadership in general; so, what makes them especially relevant to *academic* leadership? And if, as we saw in chapter 1, there have been books about mindful leadership at the elementary and secondary levels of education, why has higher education been slower to embrace this approach?

The answers to these questions can be found in the distinctive organizational culture found at colleges and universities, combined with the fact that most leadership approaches studied and adopted by administrators today developed in organizational cultures very different from our own.

THE BIMODAL UNIVERSITY

Let's begin by recognizing that most colleges and universities are structured as *bimodal organizations*. In other words, they operate with two very different organizational cultures existing side by side.

The nonacademic side of a university tends to be largely hierarchical. In a traditional hierarchy, power increases as one moves up the ranks; numbers of people increase as you move down the ranks. The result is a *social pyramid*. (See figure 6.1.) There's one CEO (chief executive officer) with the most power in the entire organization, several vice presidents with a great deal of power, even more directors with some power, and so on until you reach the rank of employees who have relatively little power although they are large in number.

Figure 6.1 Hierarchical Organizations or Social Pyramids. *Source:* Author.

That same power structure can be found in the military (commander in chief, generals, colonels, lieutenants, and so on), as well as at colleges and universities in such areas as business affairs, student affairs, development, community outreach, and similar areas. The "chain of command" tends to be very important in this type of organizational culture, and initiatives are usually begun by the upper levels of the hierarchy and implemented by the lower levels.

If you look at the organizational charts of most colleges and universities, the academic side of the institution would appear to function in much the same way. Faculty members report to chairs, who in turn report to deans, who then report to the provost, who (like other vice presidents) reports to the president or chancellor.

The problem is that the way in which initiatives are developed and carried out in academic affairs doesn't always follow this model very well. For example, major curricular changes are rarely, if ever, begun at the upper levels of the hierarchy, and even promotion recommendations almost always start at the departmental level, swimming like salmon against the stream *up* the hierarchy instead of flowing downward.

The reason for this apparent anomaly is that a hierarchical model doesn't explain very well how decisions are made or work is actually performed on the academic side of a college or university. Many decisions are made by committees where each member has an equal vote, regardless of rank or title. Rather than hierarchical organizations, therefore, many academic units and work groups function as *decentralized organizations*, where everyone is equidistant from power, and action can only be taken when consensus is achieved or a majority of the members "pool their shared power" and thus enable the group to move forward. (See figure 6.2.)

In other ways, however, institutions of higher education also work as *distributed organizations*, with different parts of the organization holding different types of power. (See figure 6.3.) To most people, the most familiar example of

Organic, Positive, and Authentic Mindfulness

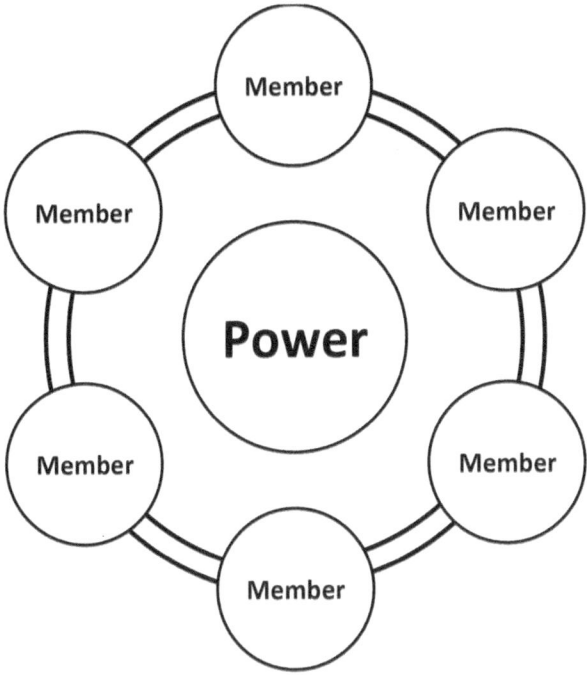

Figure 6.2 **Decentralized Organizations.** *Source:* Author.

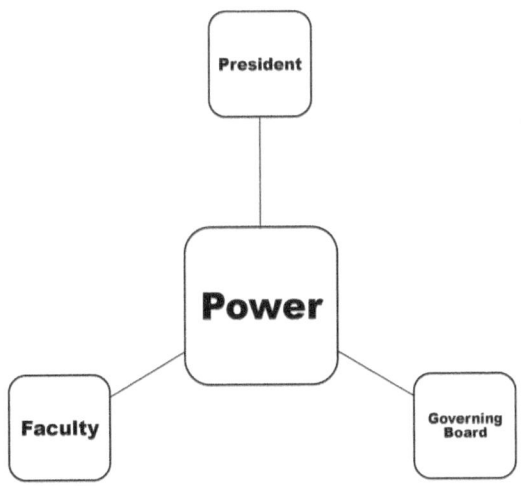

Figure 6.3 **Distributed Organizations.** *Source:* Author.

a distributed organization is the United States federal government, where the executive, legislative, and judicial branches all have their individual spheres of authority. That type of *balance of power* is reflected in the *shared governance* of colleges and universities where the governing board, administration, and faculty have separate responsibilities and spheres of authority.

That's why curricular decisions seem to flow contrary to the idea of how a hierarchy should work: The curriculum is clearly within the domain of the faculty at most institutions; it develops and revises academic programs, subject only to the approval of the administration or board in much the same way that the U.S. federal legislature creates laws, which the executive branch could veto (unless that veto is overridden) and the judicial branch could declare unconstitutional. In either case, however, creation of the law begins with Congress, and creation of the curriculum begins with the faculty.

If all of this were not confusing enough, there are also ways in which the faculty at a college or university sometimes act as a *modified matrix organization*. (See figure 6.4.) In a true matrix organization, responsibilities are formally set both horizontally and vertically. Thus a manager of marketing might report to a director who reports to a vice president (up the hierarchy) but also have responsibilities to other managers (of, for example, purchasing, research and development, production, and so on) for a specific project.

In higher education, we rarely find this type of formal cross-divisional structure, but you do find *informal* dependence on the expertise of others across academic affairs. Thus, on an institution-wide promotion committee,

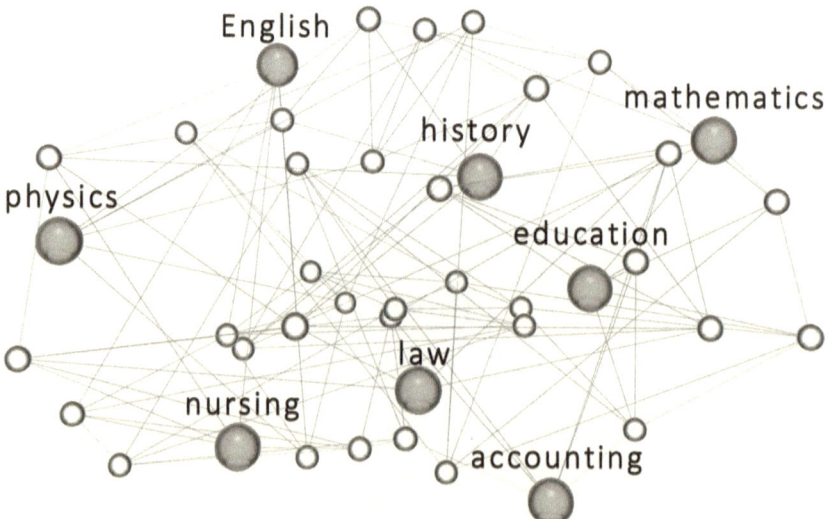

Figure 6.4 Modified Matrix Organizations. *Source:* Presenter Media.

a professor of physics may defer to a professor of English when voting on a candidate in the humanities because the latter has specialized knowledge of the field that the former doesn't have. Similarly, at an institution-wide budget hearing, a dean whose academic specialty is history may defer to a dean whose academic specialty is nursing when it comes to such matters as how large a new nursing facility should be.

Once again, the latter has specialized knowledge that the former doesn't have. But since this process occurs informally rather than as a formal organizational design, the result is a *modified* matrix culture.

THE EFFECT OF ORGANIZATIONAL CULTURE ON LEADERSHIP

The reason why it's important to understand this bimodal nature of the university is that, if we try to lead as though we're in a hierarchy when the culture we're actually operating in is decentralized, distributed, or acting as a modified matrix, we're likely to fail. And most of the books that academic leaders turn to when they're trying to improve their leadership were written by people who are experts in corporate or military culture, not academic culture.

These books thus advocate a data-driven (even, at times, data-obsessed) approach to leadership that simply ignores the reality of what it's like to work with actual faculty members today. They emphasize to leaders the importance of being decisive, taking charge of situations, articulating a clear and compelling vision, and establishing a formal chain of command. Other books claim that leaders are only effective when they embrace specific values—such as courage, perseverance, duty, and the like—regardless of the leader's own personality or the perspectives of the faculty, staff, students, and other stakeholders in the institution.

The result is that academic leaders sometimes try to act as though their colleges and departments were corporations, battalions, or athletic teams, creating a rift between faculty and administration that doesn't need to exist. Think, for instance, of the qualities that often make someone a successful entrepreneur: The person may be dogged in the pursuit of a particular goal, insistent that the organization he or she creates reflect a certain set of corporate values, and almost dictatorial in demanding that each division of the organization operate in a specific way and that the products or services produced adhere to exacting standards.

That type of leadership can work well in a social pyramid where all power and authority becomes increasingly concentrated at each higher level of the hierarchy until it culminates in a single individual. But if someone tried to lead that way in a decentralized organization (where power is shared), a distributed organization (where different powers are allocated to different divisions), or a modified matrix organization (where the tradition is that people defer to others on issues where their professional expertise is singularly relevant), the result is likely to be a disaster.

The person would be trying to accomplish tasks in a manner that runs contrary to how that system works. People may tolerate it in the short term. But in the longer term, there's likely to be passive-aggressive behavior, disengagement, or even open rebellion.

Leaders in higher education thus could apply the lessons they learn from leadership books written by experts in corporate, military, or athletic environments, but only on the nonacademic side of the institution. There, the more hierarchical organizational culture makes this "top-down" style of management not only effective, but often expected.

On the academic side of the institution, however, those same leadership strategies are likely to be counterproductive. A new president, provost, or dean who enters his or her position with an authoritative mindset is likely to accomplish a few things during his or her first year of administration (when most new leaders have a "honeymoon period," particularly if the most recent person in that position was not widely admired) and even during his or her second year (when people are still trying to figure out what the administrator's long-term goals are), but his or her strategies typically collapse in about the third year.

It's sort of like playing chess with a child who believes that the game is the same as checkers: The first few moves may look satisfactory, even somewhat reasonable. It's only as the game continues that you suddenly realize that the other person is playing by rules that don't apply to the game.

Mindful academic leadership thus helps administrators become more effective because it prepares them to remain aware of what actually happens while it is still happening and not to make premature judgments about what *should* be happening. Instead of trying to impose an authoritarian approach to leadership that runs contrary to the organizational culture of academic units, mindful leaders remain more nimble in their ability to respond to challenges and opportunities by having three additional leadership approaches in their administrative toolkits.

Although they can be authoritative and decisive when that approach is called for, they can also adopt one or more of the following alternative approaches to leadership:

- *Organic academic leadership* is the higher education equivalent of what is often referred to as *servant leadership*. Traditionally in servant leadership, leaders assume their roles not out of a desire for wealth, control, or the other common attributes of power, but out of a sense of commitment to others in the organization. Leaders, in short, view themselves as serving those who report to them, not commanding or ruling them (Wheeler 2012). In higher education, however, the metaphor of administrators as *servants* (which can be misinterpreted to mean that members of the faculty, staff, parent groups, and student body are the actual *masters* in the organization, while the administration only implements their desires) is not always helpful or appropriate. For this reason, the term *organic academic leadership* is preferable because it conveys the image of the administrator as a gardener who cares for the soil in which flowers, plants, and trees (i.e., the stakeholders of a college or university) can flourish and bear fruit (Buller 2015, 217–39). In organic academic leadership, administrators don't see their role as establishing a vision for the institution and then demanding that others pursue it. Instead, they see their task as working to develop a rich, creative environment in which the best ideas will develop organically from the groundwork they have prepared.

- *Positive academic leadership* involves working with others collegially to identify the best possible outcome in any situation and then devoting all one's energy to make that outcome a reality. As a leadership approach, it is positive in the sense that it doesn't waste opportunities by focusing on assigning blame, regretting past decisions, or fearing what might (but probably won't) occur. Nevertheless, positive academic leadership shouldn't be confused with blind optimism, the power of positive thinking, or maintaining a cheery demeanor in the face of genuine disasters. Rather, it means that leaders are capable of distinguishing *genuine* disasters from situations that are merely inconvenient or that disturb them personally because they don't coincide with their particular worldview. Instead of fixating on problems, positive academic leaders direct their attention to what's working. They take a systems-oriented approach, understanding how the distinctive components of their programs function synergistically instead of insisting that every program and every person be exactly alike. And they view themselves as coaches and mentors instead of arbiters, managers, or judges (Buller 2013).

- *Authentic academic leadership* begins with the identification of one's personal core values and then seeks to develop a leadership style that accurately and consistently reflects those values. As opposed to virtue-based leadership approaches (such as those presented in Haden and Jenkins 2016, and Williams and Kerasotis 2015), authentic academic leadership doesn't insist that there is a specific set of virtues that an effective leader must have. Rather, it encourages each leader to reflect on his or her own nature and motivations, as socially unpopular and self-servicing as they may be, and develop a leadership approach that improves the program or institution while still embodying his or her actual values. For example, laziness can be transformed into a leadership advantage if it is applied to a search for the easiest and most efficient ways of accomplishing important goals. Being self-centered can be transformed into a leadership advantage if one uses a desire for personal admiration and gain to act in ways that also bring acclaim and additional resources to the institution. A tendency toward anger can be transformed into a leadership advantage if it is channeled as righteous indignation about injustices, negligence, and long overdue changes that must be made. Authentic academic leadership recognizes that hypocrisy and inauthenticity are critical failings in the academic world, an environment where scholarly integrity is fundamental to everything we do. As soon as members of the faculty and staff recognize that an academic leader's statements of high moral principles are nothing but platitudes and that his or her pretense of virtue is merely a façade, they lose confidence in that leader to such an extent that it can't be restored. Therefore, although it may initially seem counterintuitive, academic leaders are often more effective when they are candid sinners than when they are hypocritical saints.

Mindful academic leadership is not at all identical to organic, positive, or authentic academic leadership, but it can provide a framework that supports any or all of these approaches.

By increasing our awareness of experience as it is unfolding, we're more likely to see the people we work with as ends in themselves, not means to an end, and thus lead more organically. By remaining conscious of the present moment instead of regretting the past and worrying about the future, we're more likely to lead more positively. And by taking the time to reflect on who we really are instead of always strategizing about the best ways to accomplish this or that goal, we're more likely to lead more authentically. And in the complex, often non-hierarchical culture of academic life, the result is that we'll lead more effectively.

LEADING WITH POSITIVE DEFAULT

The stereotypical image of the leader is someone who has to "ride herd" over others in the organization and prevent them from contributing only mediocre work and placing their own personal satisfaction ahead of the organization's goals. In 1960, Douglas McGregor, a management professor at MIT who later went on to become the president of Antioch College, referred to this type of supervisor as a Theory X boss, someone who believed that workers were inherently

- lazy,
- passive,
- lacking in ambition,
- resistant to change, and
- sheep needing to be led.

By contrast, McGregor found that a different type of supervisor, which he called a Theory Y boss, was often more effective. This type of leader trusts people to be

- motivated,
- interested in their work,
- ambitious,
- eager to become leaders themselves, and
- interested in change. (McGregor 1960)

About twenty years after McGregor, William Ouchi, the Sanford and Betty Sigoloff Chair in Corporate Renewal at the UCLA Anderson School of Management, described a third category of leader, which he characterized as a Theory Z boss. Theory Z bosses care about employees as individuals, make as many decisions as possible collectively, and trust workers to know their own jobs better than anyone else (Ouchi 1981).

The big difference between Theory X bosses and their Theory Y and Z counterparts is found in the area of trust. Theory X leaders don't trust their followers; they feel they have to control people in order to achieve what's best for their organizations. Theory Y and Z leaders understand that very few people make mistakes *intentionally*. When someone's work is less than satisfactory, it's rarely because of malice or desire. Other factors, including factors that extend far beyond the workplace, are usually behind the poor performance.

Successful academic leaders usually practice what is called *positive default*: the assumption that the vast majority of people are really just trying to do what's best (Buller and Cipriano 2015, 65). Mindfulness can be a great way of increasing positive default in leaders.

As Michael Carroll states in *The Mindful Leader*, "[M]indful leadership is tremendously practical because it rests on a simple yet profound insight that expands the entire notion of leadership altogether: *all human beings instinctively want to offer their best to others and in turn inspire others to do the same, and this can be done by anyone, anywhere, anytime*" (Carroll 2011, 18; emphasis in original). The more we engage in mindfulness, therefore, the more likely we are to trust those we work with. In addition, we become more likely to inspire them to become trusting leaders themselves.

LEADING BY INSPIRATION

Because mindful academic leaders take the time to know both themselves and the people they work with, they are more likely to lead by inspiration than are leaders who become so preoccupied by goals and metrics that they view people merely as instruments for achieving their objectives.

Janice Marturano distinguishes leading by inspiration from other approaches that supervisors might take in the following manner:

> [A] common way we fail to lead with excellence is managing by expectation rather than leading by inspiration. When we lead with excellence, our primary responsibility is to inspire those around us, knowing that if a capable employee is genuinely motivated, and he or she understands the ultimate goals, there is no need to micromanage. (Marturano 2015, 130)

In Marturano's view, we manage by expectation when we force people into pigeonholes, failing to perceive them as fully three-dimensional human beings or being unable to imagine them in any other positions than the ones they already hold. We also manage by expectation when we're overly prescriptive about how people are supposed to perform their work, dictating specifications and not empowering them to become more independent.

When we lead by inspiration, we act as mentors and role models rather than taskmasters, sharing our principles—or even "our mantras"—with our stakeholders so that they understand our core values, and we delegate authority, not merely responsibility. Leading by inspiration thus permits effective succession planning because it's not dependent on one irreplaceable "boss" who plans and controls everyone's actions but instead permits a great deal of cross-training, independence, and professional growth.

As a way of summarizing many of the benefits we have explored throughout this discussion, we might turn to what Ray Williams, a leadership trainer and executive coach, calls the *Seven Habits of Highly Mindful Leaders* (Williams 2016). In Williams's view, highly mindful leaders

1. Remain grounded in the present. "[S]pending too much time thinking about the future can result in a leader missing what exists in the present or being closed-minded to different possibilities that exist in the present."
2. Develop emotional intelligence because they engage in regular, introspective self-awareness. Achieving this goal involves "taking the time in the present to reflect on one's inner thoughts; being aware and accepting one's emotional state as it occurs; regularly connecting with one's personal purpose in life; and taking the time for quiet reflection alone, in silence, unencumbered by interruptions."

3. Are aware of their own energy cycles and rhythms, knowing which times of day are best for them to engage in intellectual tasks, interpersonal tasks, or physical tasks. "Managing energy, not time, is a key to enduring optimal performance for highly mindful leaders. This includes managing one's mental and emotional energy, not just physical energy."
4. Respond intentionally rather than react automatically. "Highly mindful leaders demonstrate an ability to slow down, being conscious of their breathing, observing carefully what is going on in their internal emotional state, and then making a conscious intentional decision to respond."
5. Act with generosity and understanding. "Highly mindful leaders demonstrate [acceptance and compassion] through their interactions with others; not only through empathy and restraint in judgment and criticism, but also through acceptance of and compassion for others, a desire to create a humanistic work culture, one in which the well-being of self and others thrives."
6. Demonstrate openness. "This habit involves not only being open to varying ideas and perspectives of others, which generally involves cognitive processes, but also practicing what is known as 'beginner's mind,' or approaching each person, event and situation as though one had never experienced that before."
7. Practice non-attachment. "Highly mindful leaders can have a desired vision of the future and general notion on how to get there, but realize a narrow and rigid attachment to specific outcomes often results in disappointment and blame for 'failures' when those outcomes don't occur." (Williams 2016)

Awareness of self and others, generosity, openness, intentionality, and non-attachment are the very qualities that develop over time through shamatha, vipassana, mantra, and metta meditation or the non-meditative alternatives we've explored in this text. They are also the qualities that help one lead most effectively in the highly complex organizational culture of higher education.

THE VUCA WORLD

One expression that originated in the highly hierarchical culture of the military has rapidly been embraced by other organizational structures as well: the VUCA World. This expression is a shorthand way of signifying that the world in which we act is *Volatile, Uncertain, Complex,* and *Ambiguous*. The most common advice for operating in the VUCA World is to remain aware of one's environment at all times and prepared to change course immediately should the situation require it. In short, one should practice mindful leadership.

That mindful approach is singularly important in the VUCA World that characterizes so much of modern higher education. We're working in an environment in which there are serious disagreements about the very purpose of colleges and universities. Is our goal to prepare people for jobs, produce well-rounded citizens, or something else?

We're working in an environment in which our stakeholders are demanding mutually exclusive results. Should we keep costs low, preserve low student-to-faculty ratios, or provide the type of campus amenities that most students have come to expect?

We're working in an environment in which our future is still very unclear, and yet we're required to plan strategically for this indistinct future. It's no wonder that we feel that our professional environment is volatile, uncertain, complex, and ambiguous.

If that academic context takes a toll on us, it affects our other stakeholders as well. Members of the faculty, staff, student body, and community, as well as parents and donors, are likely to find themselves increasingly frustrated by institutions that seem to demand more of them while offering less personal attention and concern for them as individuals.

Mindful academic leadership helps us deal more effectively with these concerns as well. The greater awareness and generosity it brings allows us to understand the struggles that others face and realize that, when their exasperation boils over into anger toward us, it isn't really us they're upset with; what bothers them are the same situations that often bother us. And to the extent that we can see ourselves as all in the same predicament, we have a better chance of addressing the problems that concern the entire academic community.

THE LAST STEP

In chapter 1, you completed an inventory (table 1.1) that assessed your current level of mindless, automatic response to things that occurred and then were urged to examine other such inventories as the Freiburg Mindfulness Inventory, the Mindful Attention Awareness Scale, and the Toronto Mindfulness Scale.

Now that you've completed this book and practiced at least some of the activities recommended in it, go back and take these inventories again. You're likely to find that your mindless, automatic responses have decreased and your mindful awareness of experience as it occurs has increased. That's an important step toward increasing the effectiveness of your academic leadership and providing you with additional tools in your administrative toolkit.

If you'd like to continue your journey further, consider exploring some of the resources that are presented at the end of each chapter, signing up for formal training in meditation or mindfulness-based stress reduction, or starting your own support group for mindful leaders on your campus. Even a small cohort of mindful leaders can make a noticeable improvement in the quality of higher education.

KEY POINTS FROM CHAPTER 6

- Colleges and universities have highly bimodal organizational cultures in that leadership proceeds in a hierarchical or top-down manner in most non-academic units but in a far more complex manner (combining elements of hierarchical, decentralized, distributed, and modified matrix organizational cultures) on the academic side of the institution.
- That complexity means that leadership in academic units is often ineffective when it proceeds in an authoritarian manner. Alternative approaches such as servant or organic leadership, positive leadership, and authentic leadership tend to serve the needs of academic units better.
- Mindful academic leadership gives administrators the awareness and understanding they need in order to adopt the most effective leadership approach in each individual situation.
- Mindful academic leaders seek to lead by inspiration rather than manage by expectation.
- Ray Williams's Seven Habits of Highly Mindful Leaders provides a useful survey of the benefits produced by mindful academic leadership.
- Mindful leadership better prepares administrators for functioning in what has been termed a VUCA (volatile, uncertain, complex, and ambiguous) World.

REFERENCES

Buller, J. L. 2013. *Positive Academic Leadership: How to Stop Putting Out Fires and Start Making a Difference.* San Francisco: Jossey-Bass.

Buller, J. L. 2015. *Change Leadership in Higher Education: A Practical Guide to Academic Transformation.* San Francisco: Jossey-Bass.

Buller, J. L., and R. E. Cipriano. 2015. *A Toolkit for College Professors.* Lanham, MD: Rowman & Littlefield.

Carroll, M. 2011. *The Mindful Leader: Awakening Your Natural Management Skills through Mindfulness Meditation.* Boston: Trumpeter.

Haden, N. K., and R. Jenkins. 2016. *The 9 Virtues of Exceptional Leaders: Unlocking Your Leadership Potential* (2nd ed.). Atlanta, GA: Deeds.

Marturano, J. 2015. *Finding the Space to Lead: A Practical Guide to Mindful Leadership.* New York: Bloomsbury.

McGregor, D. 1960. *The Human Side of Enterprise.* New York: McGraw-Hill.

Ouchi, W. G. 1981. *Theory Z: How American Business Can Meet the Japanese Challenge.* Reading, MA: Addison-Wesley.

Wheeler, D. W. 2012. *Servant Leadership for Higher Education: Principles and Practices.* San Francisco: Jossey-Bass.

Williams, P., and P. Kerasotis. 2015. *Extreme Winning: 12 Keys to Unlocking the Winner within You.* Deerfield Beach, FL: Health Communications.

Williams, R. 2016. "The 7 Habits of Highly Mindful Leaders." *International Coaching Federation,* August 10, 2016. Retrieved from https://coachfederation.org/blog/the-7-habits-of-highly-mindful-leaders.

RESOURCES

Abouserie, R. 1996. "Stress, Coping Strategies and Job Satisfaction in University Academic Staff." *Educational Psychology* 16 (1): 49–56.

David, S. 2016. *Emotional Agility: Get Unstuck, Embrace Change, and Thrive in Work and Life.* Garden City, NY: Avery.

Maravelas, A. 2005. *How to Reduce Workplace Conflict and Stress: How Leaders and Their Employees Can Protect Their Sanity and Productivity from Tension and Turf Wars.* Pompton Plains, NJ: The Career Press, Inc.

Scott, S. J., and B. Davenport. 2016. *Declutter Your Mind: How to Stop Worrying, Relieve Anxiety, and Eliminate Negative Thinking.* Cranbury, NJ: Oldtown Publishing LLC.

Wells, C. M. 2016. *Mindfulness: How School Leaders Can Reduce Stress and Thrive on the Job.* Lanham, MD: Rowman & Littlefield.

About the Author

Jeffrey L. Buller has served in administrative positions ranging from department chair to vice president for academic affairs at four very different institutions: Loras College, Georgia Southern University, Mary Baldwin College, and Florida Atlantic University. He is the author of seventeen books on higher education administration, a textbook for first-year college students, and a book of essays on the music dramas of Richard Wagner. Dr. Buller has also written numerous articles on Greek and Latin literature, nineteenth- and twentieth-century opera, and college administration. From 2003 to 2005, he served as the principal English-language lecturer at the International Wagner Festival in Bayreuth, Germany. More recently, he has been active as a consultant to the Ministry of Education in Saudi Arabia, where he is assisting with the creation of a kingdom-wide Academic Leadership Center. Along with Robert E. Cipriano, Dr. Buller is a senior partner in ATLAS: Academic Training, Leadership, & Assessment Services, through which he has presented numerous workshops on mindful academic leadership and developing more effective strategies for higher education administration.

More about ATLAS

ATLAS: Academic Training, Leadership, & Assessment Services offers training programs, books, and materials dealing with collegiality and positive academic leadership. Its more than fifty highly interactive programs include the following:

- Introduction to Academic Leadership
- Team Building for Academic Leaders
- Time Management for Academic Leaders
- Stress Management for Academic Leaders
- Budgeting for Academic Leaders
- Decision Making for Academic Leaders
- Problem Solving for Academic Leaders
- Conflict Management for Academic Leaders
- Emotional Intelligence for Academic Leaders
- Effective Communication for Academic Leaders
- Career Development for College Professors

- Best Practices in Academic Fundraising
- The Introvert's Guide to Academic Leadership
- Work-Life Balance
- Shared Governance: Only a Catchphrase?
- Succession Planning in Higher Education
- Motivation: How to Spur Yourself and Others on to Greater Things
- The Art of Small Talk: What Do I Say When I Fear I Have Nothing to Say?
- Developing Leadership Capacity: How You Can Create a Leadership Development Program at Your Institution
- We've Got to Stop Meeting Like This: Leading Meetings Effectively
- Protect Yourself from a Toxic Work Environment
- Why Academic Leaders Must Lead Differently: Understanding the Organizational Culture of Higher Education
- Getting Organized: Taking Control of Your Schedule, Workspace, and Habits to Get More Done in Less Time with Lower Stress
- Collegiality and Teambuilding
- Change Leadership in Higher Education
- Promoting Faculty and Staff Engagement
- Best Practices in Faculty Recruitment and Hiring
- Best Practices in Faculty Evaluation
- Best Practices in Coaching and Mentoring
- Moving Forward: Training and Development for Advisory Boards
- Training the Trainers: How to Give Presentations and Provide Training the ATLAS Way
- Managing Up for Academic Leaders: How to Flourish When Dealing with Your Boss and Your Boss's Boss
- Creating a Culture of Student Success
- Positive Academic Leadership: How to Stop Putting Out Fires and Start Making a Difference
- Authentic Academic Leadership: A Values-Based Approach to Academic Leadership
- Mindful Academic Leadership: A Mindfulness-Based Approach to Academic Leadership
- Fostering a Collegial University: An In-Depth Exploration of Collegiality in Higher Education
- Managing Conflict: An In-Depth Exploration of Conflict Management in Higher Education
- A Toolkit for College Professors
- A Toolkit for Department Chairs
- Exploring Academic Leadership: Is College/University Administration Right for Me?

ATLAS offers programs in half-day, full-day, and multi-day formats. ATLAS also offers reduced prices on leadership books and sells materials that can be used to assess your institution or program:

- the Collegiality Assessment Matrix (CAM), which allows academic programs to evaluate the collegiality and civility of their faculty members in a consistent, objective, and reliable manner
- the Self-Assessment Matrix (S-AM), which is a self-evaluation version of the CAM
- the ATLAS Campus Climate and Morale Survey
- the ATLAS Faculty and Staff Engagement Survey

These assessment instruments are available in both electronic and paper formats. In addition, the ATLAS E-Newsletter addresses a variety of issues related to academic leadership and is sent free to subscribers.

For more information, contact:
ATLAS: Academic Training, Leadership, & Assessment Services
9154 Wooden Road
Raleigh, NC 27617
Telephone: 1 (800) 355-6742
Email: questions@atlasleadership.com
Website: www.atlasleadership.com

www.ingramcontent.com/pod-product-compliance
Lightning Source LLC
Chambersburg PA
CBHW030143240426
43672CB00005B/249